Zoence®–the
Science of Life

Zoence®–the Science of Life

Discovering the Sacred Spaces of Your Life

Peter Dawkins

SAMUEL WEISER, INC.

York Beach, Maine

First published in the USA in 1998 by
Samuel Weiser, Inc.
P. O. Box 612
York Beach, ME 03910-0612

Library of Congress Cataloging-in-Publication Data

Dawkins, Peter.
    Zoence®—the science of life : discovering the sacred spaces of your
life / Peter Dawkins.
        p.   cm.
    Originally published: U[nited] K[ingdom] : Wigmore Publications,
1995.
    ISBN 1-57863-042-8 (alk. paper)
    1. Spiritual life—Miscellanea. 2. Sacred space—Miscellanea.
3. Life—Miscellanea. I. Title.
BF1999.D327   1998
128—dc21   98-24636
                                                                CIP

MG

Typeset in 10 pt. Bembo

Printed in the United States of America

05 04 03 02 01 00 99 98
10 9 8 7 6 5 4 3 2 1

Dedicated in love to Sarah

When the love, the lover and the beloved have become one, when we see God and love him as the innermost Self in all beings, and when there is a continuous current of love flowing in the heart, then it is that we realize divine love.
—SRIMAD BHAGAVATUM

Contents

List of Illustrations

Color plates are found between pages 43 and 58.

Acknowledgments

The author wishes to acknowledge with gratitude all those who have helped make this publication possible, and in particular the Gatekeeper Trust, the Francis Bacon Research Trust, the Merlyn Trust, Michelle Beaufort, Gay Browning, Anthea Courtney, Irene Dalichow, Sarah Dawkins, John Dawkins, Samuel Dawkins, Jill Line, Almut Martini, Francis McKeagney, Dominic McManus, Diana Myers, Mary Pout, Marianne Rieke, Suzie Straw, Sue Taylor, Diana Tinson, Geralyn Walsh, Mary Walsh, Dickie Wilson and Robert Wilson.

Diagrams by Samuel Dawkins and Michelle Beaufort.

Photographs by the author unless otherwise stated. Other photographs by John Dawkins, Dominic McManus, Marianne Rieke, Suzie Straw, and Sue Taylor.

Illustrations reproduced by kind permission of The National Gallery, London (Raphael's "Crucifixion"), and The British Library, London (Title-page of the 1611 A.V. Bible).

Figures 39, 40, 41, 42, 43, 44 and 45 use Mountain High Map images. (Mountain High Maps® Copyright © 1993 Digital Wisdom, Inc.)

Quoted material at chapter openings comes from the following sources:

page v:
Srimad Bhagavatum, *The Wisdom of God,* Swami Prabhavananda, trans. (Sri Ramakrishna Math, Madras, 1972), p. 51;

chapter 1:
William Blake, *The Marriage of Heaven and Hell* in *The Collected Works of William Blake,* Geoffrey Keynes, ed. London: Nonesuch Press, 1927; 4th edition, 1975), p. 182;

chapter 2:
Llywelyn Sion, *The Book of Bardism,* Quoted in Lewis Spence, *The Mysteries of Britain* (London: Rider & Co., 1928), p. 96;

chapter 3:
Ovid, *Metamorphoses*, Book XV: *The Teachings of Pythagoras*, Frank Justus Miller, trans. (London: William Heinemann, Ltd., 1951);

chapter 4:
Manly P. Hall, *Man, the Grand Symbol of the Mysteries* (Los Angeles: Philosophical Research Society, 1972), p. 154;

chapter 5:
Alexander Pope, "Essay on Man," in *Pope: Poetical Works,* Herbert Davis, ed. (London: Oxford University Press 1978), Epistle 1, l 267–268;

chapter 6:
Hildegard von Bingen, in *Meditations with Hildegard of Bingen,* Introduction and versions by Gabriele Uhlein (Santa Fe, NM: Bear & Co., 1983), pp. 58–61;

chapter 7:
Hildegard von Bingen, in *Meditations with Hildegard of Bingen,* p. 49;

chapter 8:
Sri Yukteswar, Sutras 1 & 2, *Kailya Darsanam* ("Exposition of Final Truth"), translated by Self-Realization Fellowship, published as *The Holy Science* by Swami Sri Yukteswar (Los Angeles: Self-Realization Fellowship, 1984); and *page 144*: The Taittirya Upanishad 3. 1–6, from *The Upanishads,* p. 111. Translations from the Sanskrit with an introduction by Juan Mascaro (London: Penguin, 1965).

Introduction—
What is Zoence?

Zoence is a complete philosophy and practical science of life. It is a science of living in harmony with ourselves and our environment, and of uniting Earth with Heaven, Heaven with Earth. The practice of Zoence enhances our lives and all that we do, bringing joy and fulfillment.

Zoence can be summed up as knowing the right thing to do in the right place, at the right time, and with the right orientation. It is based on natural laws and principles which, when successfully applied, bring balance, health, prosperity, and happiness to both human beings and nature.

Known and practiced in various degrees by the more enlightened cultures and societies from the most ancient times, Zoence is a modern development based upon the underlying wisdom common to the various wisdom traditions of the West, and which has its parallels in Eastern philosophy and practice. Zoence goes to the heart and root of the many wisdom traditions, synthesizing them and drawing on their essence. It presents the basic truths with new discoveries and insights for the world of today and tomorrow.

The Greek word *Zoe* means "life," and Zoence is a science of life concerning ourselves, our environment, our planet and the cosmos. Its basic philosophy is that life, itself, is fundamentally good and is meant for enjoyment, but that we ourselves have to discover how to enjoy life and to give joy to life. Zoence is founded upon love, recognizing love as the basis of all true life which leads to self-knowledge and joy.

Practicing the principles of Zoence in everyday life can enhance our abilities in all areas, bringing increasing good health, harmony and happiness. Zoence helps us to develop our sensitivity, our awareness and our perception. It also helps us to develop harmony with other people, with our environment and with nature. Moreover, it empowers us in all that we do.

Zoence is based on the principle that humanity is an integral part of the whole: therefore our environment affects our consciousness, and our consciousness affects the environment. Consciousness in turn leads to behavior. To live in harmony with ourselves and our environment involves much more than learning to live peaceably with each other without polluting the Earth that supports us, the water we drink, or the very air we breathe.

Even if we are not aware of it, we are constantly affected by our surroundings, which can cause illness, depression, and disturbed behavior—or, alternatively, can create and maintain good physical and emotional health, and creativity. By the same token, our emotions, thoughts, and actions affect the environment for good or ill. Zoence teaches how we can, with conscious awareness, bring greater harmony and health to the planet, while at the same time benefiting our own lives.

Zoence is a modern Western equivalent of the ancient Chinese *Feng Shui,* which is, among other things, the art and science of harmonious relationships within the environment. Always recognized as of vital importance in the East, nowadays *Feng Shui* is becoming increasingly popular in the West: even the business world is becoming aware of the influence of architecture and the environment on health, harmony, and the ability to prosper.

Zoence, like *Feng Shui,* is also about much more than the placing and design of buildings. It is about the relationship between Heaven and Earth, mind and matter. In China, *Feng Shui* has both a religious and philosophical role, as well as being a practical science of life. The name itself means "Wind-Water," echoing the Biblical account of Creation: "The Spirit (Breath) of God moved upon the face of the Waters" (Genesis 1:2). The two polarities, the wind of heaven and the waters of the earth, or spirit and matter, creativity and receptivity, interact in a continual and loving act of creation.

Through the practice of Zoence we can assist in this process, so that both we and the planet can evolve toward a greater beauty and expression of our divine potential.

Zoence has also been called "The Temple Science." Beautiful and harmonious forms are known as temples. Our own bodies can be temples, as can be our homes, offices, and environment. Likewise, the landscape of nature and of the Earth, itself, can be seen as a temple.

The world about us and the bodies we inhabit are basically structures of energy. The whole Universe is composed of energy. All structures of energy constitute architecture, whether manmade or natural; and when we build houses, towns, cities, gardens, and parks, we create an interrelationship that forms a structure. Carried out correctly and harmoniously, this reflects the structure of the Cosmos, which is a network of light and energy disposed in exquisite but ever-moving patterns of beauty, underlying which is a wonderful order and harmony.

Many people today are familiar with the concept of chakras, the energy centers within the body which for good health need to be in a state of balance and flow. Similarly, the landscape around us, the planet and the Universe are structures of energy, with various interrelated systems of chakras and energy lines.

There are particular areas of the landscape that show complete systems of chakras and which have energy structures analogous to that which underlies the human body. In Zoence these are known as landscape temples. There are both small and large ones, the smaller lying within the larger. For example, every chakra of a large landscape temple is, itself, a smaller landscape temple with its own set of chakras. Understanding the principles of Zoence enables us to work with and enhance these power-points of the Earth, to benefit both ourselves and nature.

We have the power to destroy and pollute nature—but we also have the power to energize and heal it, to keep it wholesome and to enhance its natural beauty and prosperity. Zoence teaches us how to do this, through paying attention to our surroundings and rediscovering our ability to heal the land through right living and through such things as practicing the ancient art of pilgrimage. This is healing and invigorating for us, since we are essentially part of nature, and whatever we do to nature we do to ourselves.

Pilgrimage—a journey through a landscape or a visit to a special place, undertaken with a loving awareness of the sanctity of life and of the place, and with a dedicated good intention—works with the energy currents and chakras of the Earth in such a way as to stimulate healing and transmutation. Pilgrimages have always been and still are major features of all the great cultures and religions of the world, as well as of private individuals on their own personal quest for truth. When performed well, as an art, pilgrimage can be equated with acupressure on the energy meridians and acupuncture points of the world, as well as with cleansing and reinvigorating the Earth's circulatory system. It is a way of giving both healing and increased vitality through love and illumined consciousness to the chakras and nervous system of the planetary body.

At the same time the pilgrim, who naturally becomes more receptive to the great blessings which nature and our environment can give to us, is in turn cleansed and healed, reinvigorated and inspired. This, and other Zoence practices, builds up what might be called the Affectionate Alliance—friendship between people, and friendship between people and their environment.

The laws of energy apply not only to our physical and psychological environment—the space in which we dwell—but also to time, with its ongoing cycles of the days, seasons, and years. Zoence teaches us how to become conscious of our own life process and the time cycles within it, together with the importance of celebrating the ancient seasonal festivals.

This book is a short introduction to some of the basic principles of Zoence, pointing out how they manifest in ourselves, in nature and our environment, and in our lives, with some practical suggestions and examples of Zoence in action.

Zoence®–the
Science of Life

ONE

The Principles of Zoence

~~~

Energy is eternal delight.
—WILLIAM BLAKE

WHAT IS LIFE?

Zoence, the science of life, is based on the understanding of energy and its relationship with life. As modern scientists recognize, the whole Universe consists of energy. Energy *is* life, for life is a flowing, moving energy that animates all things, and all things are themselves built out of this energy. Everything in creation, from rocks and mountains to plants, animals and human beings, is a living structure of energy. Moreover, this energy has a consciousness; the type of consciousness depends upon what form the energy takes. Living in harmony depends on the harmonious flow of energy between ourselves and our environment, between ourselves and other living beings, and not least, on our own inner relationship with the elements of our own self.

Like the human body, the landscape of the world is essentially a matrix of energy, as is the whole body of the planet and the Universe itself. Energy is disposed in patterns which demonstrate a remarkable order and harmony. Within these patterns are focal points, beautifully patterned radiant centers and vortices of energy known as chakras (from the Sanskrit word *chakra*, meaning "wheel").

Together with the overall energy patterns, these chakras form power points which influence whole areas of human life and consciousness as well as those of nature. They exist in all three dimensions of space and also in the fourth dimension of time. Some are more powerful than others, but each has its own quality and purpose and influence on life.

Initiate architects and sages from the most ancient times have understood a great deal about these patterns and relationships, and how they can be used to create harmony in people's lives and environment. One of the aims of Zoence is to restore this knowledge to as many people as possible, in as simple and fundamental way as possible, and to encourage its practice and further development.

LOVE AND ENERGY

Many great civilizations of antiquity were founded on a deep sense of the sacred nature of life and the environment, and an innate understanding of energy and consciousness. They shared the idea that the Universe, seen and unseen, was a harmonious creation designed by the ultimate Architect—whether you call that Architect God, the All-Good, Allah, Parabrahma, or any other name. St. John and Christianity identify the Supreme Architect, the Divine Being, as Love, as do Sufism, Buddhism, and other philosophies. Zoence takes this point of view.

The myths of creation, including the Hebraic Book of Genesis, tell us how both Heaven and Earth were originally created from the dark, formless Void. How did life and all creation come into material being out of this unmanifested state of pure potential?

In the beginning, we are told, God desired to be manifest. That desire was (and still is) the motivating force underlying all creation. Moreover, since God is Love, God's desire is all-loving. The energy of this love is the creative life force. It is always in motion, since the nature of energy is movement. It is always flowing out of the heart of the Universe, out of the heart of God, as divine E-MOTION, the creative, inspiring and motivating force of the Universe.

ALL LIFE IS POLARITY

Besides love, the concept of polarity is crucial to an understanding of life. Without polarity, in fact, nothing can exist. As sacred tradition tells us, Existence, itself, began with the two poles of existence, Heaven and Earth—the darkness and the deep: "In the beginning God created heaven and earth, and the earth was without form and void, and darkness lay upon the face of the deep."[1] When heaven became active as the "spirit of God," and Earth passive and responsive as the "waters" moved by the movement of the spirit, then Existence became manifest and creative.

The heavenly polarity is known as "spirit," or "breath," and the earthly polarity as the "waters" of matter. They are the two poles or "faces" of God—the two poles of Love—which enable love to be expressed: so that God might love God, or Love might love Love. When there is no desire, no movement and no response, then there is Nothing—No Thing: only the potential of polarity, expressed poetically and lovingly in the Scriptures as "the darkness which lay upon the face of the deep." But as soon as there is the desire to be manifest, then the two poles of that desire appear, one in an active state of movement and the other passive but responsive.

This is essentially a love-making, which the Scriptures describe poetically as "the spirit of God (*i.e.* the spirit of Love) moving upon the face of the waters."[2] In this love-making the darkness has become the spirit or breath of life, which is creative energy or movement, while the deep has become manifested as the waters of life. The waters symbolize pure formless matter, initially in a state of inertia or rest, but which is nevertheless utterly receptive, malleable, and responsive to the spirit. The love-making expresses the love relationship of the two poles of Love, and creates all forms of life as its "children."

This basic polarity, of initiating energy and responsiveness to that energy, continues to manifest in everything it creates. All life forms have polarity. For instance, in our human form we have our inner breath or spirit (echoed by the physical breath) and our outer form within which the spirit acts and which is responsive to that spirit. Our bodies themselves have polarity—four different sets of polarity in fact: top and bottom, left and right, front and back, inside and outside. It is impossible to imagine ourselves without any of these polarities. (See figure 1, page 4.)

---

[1]Genesis 1, 1-2. All biblical quotes are from *The Companion Bible*, a variation on the King James version.

[2]Genesis 1, 2.

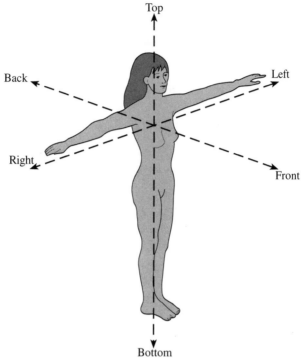

Figure 1. Polarity.

Without polarity, nothing exists. Try to imagine yourself without a top or a bottom, or without a left or right hand side, without a front or a back, or without an inside or an outside. These are the polarities of your being. Where would you be without them?

THE THREEFOLD NATURE OF LIFE

Just as nothing can exist without polarity, no two poles can exist without the relationship between them. For instance, you or I do not consist of just a top and bottom, or right and left, but also everything that lies between. Together the three form a trinity which, when in perfect harmony, is the expression of love.

The two polarities of spirit and matter are two aspects of the one Existence. Out of their relationship and interaction all forms of life are created, expressing the love and divinity of Being. Spirit and matter create the soul, the life form which manifests the divine Being. Spirit and matter are our divine parents, our soul is their child.

It is in the soul that spirit manifests itself as light. Energy takes form through its interaction with matter. As divine emotion or movement, it moves at the fastest speed possible, the speed of light, and manifests itself in matter as spiritual light: hence the word "soul," which comes from the Latin *Sol*, meaning Sun. Physical light, in which the energy-matter of the physical Universe is moving at its fastest speed possible, is a slower, less perfect version of the spiritual light which moves infinitely fast. The soul is a metaphysical or spiritual form of light, which can create for itself a physical outer form or "clothing" in which it can be incarnate.

Light is the perfect form and expression of love. From light is created the Universe and all its individual forms of life. This light or soul, which has perfect harmony and beauty, is the third aspect of the Trinity—the child of the parents. But the three are not separate; they are inseparable.

In human terms this creative principle of the trinity is expressed, for instance, when two people make a relationship of any kind. The emotional link between them is the living expression of that relationship. A good friendship, partnership, or marriage helps that energy link to develop into one of true harmony and love, which forms a metaphysical entity or expression of light and joy far greater than that of each partner alone. (By contrast, an unloving relationship characterized by fear, hatred, jealousy, or selfishness, forms a correspondingly dark entity.) The same principle can be seen working within families, communities, and nations, and between ourselves and our environment.

Energy is emotion. Creative energy, which is life, is inseparable from love. However, because we have free will, it is possible for us to have desires which are not pure or perfect; then, unless we are loving, the energy we release will not be so creatively good. Energy always flows between neighbors, whether human beings, animals, plants, hills, trees, or rivers. To develop to our full potential it is our task to be friends, not just neighbors, so that the energy which flows between us is the energy of pure love. We can develop the ability to transform that love into joy and beauty by making it conscious, and by sharing the flow of loving energy with others and the world about us in our friendship and service to each other.

Related to this matter of human potential is another polarity or trinity of great importance—strife and friendship, whose loving and balanced relationship produces harmony. Mystery schools of the past allegorized this as Mars and Venus, whose love affair resulted in the birth of Harmonia. When entering a classical temple, the pilgrim would pass between two pillars representing this polarity, with the reminder that the aim of the pilgrim was to become the true child of this love relationship—the shining, joyful, beautiful soul, Harmony. To accomplish this both strife and friendship are needed, for we release our divine potential and attain our greatest achievements by striving always for the best, but we can only truly do this in friendship, with the help of each other and all life.

Difficulties and challenges against which we strive are a great gift: without them life would be immensely boring and we would never know our own strengths or develop our inherent talents. Likewise friendship is a wonderful blessing: without friends we would be so lonely, having no one to love or be loved by, to help or to help us in our striving, or with whom to share the joy of achievement. The perverse opposite of this divine polarity, which we can bring about by means of our own desires or will, is war and enmity, wherein nothing good flourishes and nothing worthwhile is ever achieved.

RADIANT AND SPIRAL ENERGY

Energy itself has polarity. In the soul it exists as two types of energy, radiant and spiral. Radiant energy moves directly out from its center or source, in a straight line. It can move as fast as it wants without restriction. At its fastest or most perfect speed, the energy (or emotion) manifests as radiant light, or radiance.

Spiral energy spirals outwards from a center. It is also unlimited in its motion, and can gather speed until it reaches the speed of light. So spiral energy, at perfection, can manifest as light.

However, spiral energy can also spiral inward, coiling in on itself until it ultimately ties itself up into a knot and cannot move. It then becomes potential energy, or power, locked in on itself. In this unmoving state of inertia it is no longer light, but dark and invisible. This state of inert potential is associated with the darkness of pure matter; indeed, it is matter, but it is the means by which the soul can experience material forms of existence and difficulties, which in turn enable the soul to grow in self-knowledge.

For the soul to evolve in consciousness and self-knowledge, part of it has to become involved with matter. This aspect of the soul incarnates in a material body of its own making. Its energies spiral inward, trapping some of the radiance within the heart of the dark form. The soul's purpose then is to unravel its potential and release its imprisoned light and beauty, thus gaining self-knowledge and finding its joy.

Radiant energy is the polarity to spiral energy; thus the two are in a constant state of interrelationship. The two together build the form of the soul and all the different types of soul-body. At the same time they evolve the soul's consciousness or intelligence. Radiant energy, which is associated with the heavenly pole of our being, constantly interacts with the inert spirals of potential energy associated with the earthly pole of our being. Radiant energy has the power to unlock the spirals, turning them around so that they can spiral outward, freeing themselves from their inertia and enabling them to become light. In this way material life-forms evolve and gradually become spiritualized. (See figure 2, page 8.)

THE EVOLUTION OF THE SOUL

The effect of the radiant energy shining into the darkness of matter and releasing its power is symbolized in the story of St. George and the Dragon. This myth contains the secret of creation and transformation, as well as of the evolution of the soul.

Like the coiled-up dragon, every human soul has the potential to evolve from a starting point of virtual ignorance, or pure potential, into a complex and exquisitely beautiful being possessed of all knowledge. In order to evolve, the soul needs to learn how to master matter by experiencing it and working with it, so that the darkness of matter can be transformed into light.

The spear of the saint represents the spiritual ray of light piercing the dragon of matter—the sleeping, coiled-up vortex of power. Disturbed and awoken by the touch of this radiant spear, the dragon energy starts to uncoil, taking form as the dragon emerging from its lair of material darkness. As it unwinds, it gradually moves faster and faster, changing form as it does so until ultimately it is transmuted into a "soular" form of light, the beautiful princess of the myth.

In the vertical polarity of the human body and psyche, the radiant energy is associated with the crown of the head, from whence it shines down the spine, awakening the dragon-energy stored in the base of the spine (and in the Earth, itself). The dragon energy then naturally rises up the spine toward the crown. When it successfully reaches its goal,

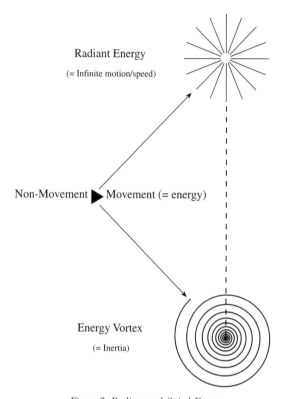

Figure 2. Radiant and Spiral Energy.

In the Indian Vedic tradition the radiant energy is associated with the three primary gods, Brahma, Vishnu and Shiva, and the spiral energy with their shaktis or consorts, the three goddesses—Saraswati, Lakshmi, and Devi. The goddesses are also known under the name of Kundalini, the dragon energy. Western tradition has a similar symbology, with the Triple Goddess, under the name of the three Marys, being the three consorts and dragon energy of the male Trinity of Father, Son, and Holy Ghost. The mythological story of St. George and the Dragon contains all this in allegorical form.

illumination of the mind and body is produced, transforming the nature of the person and bringing both harmony and joy.

The mythical description of the dragon, which can crawl on the earth, swim in water, fly in the air, and breathe fire, refers to the physical and psychological constitution of both nature and the human being—the earthiness referring to the physical body and consciousness, and the water, air and fire natures of the dragon referring to the more subtle psychological aspects. These elements (of earth, water, air, and fire) also refer to the natural process of life and to the successive transformations of consciousness brought about by the life process.

The dragon refers not only to the spiralling earth energy, but also to the materialistic and largely selfish state of an unevolved human being. The princess represents the pure or virgin soul which each human being eventually becomes, wherein the dragon nature dies and a virtuous nature is born in its stead. This is accomplished by contact with the spiritual self and its radiant energy of love. Ultimately the virgin soul becomes so united with and illumined by its spiritual self that it gives birth to (or becomes) the golden child of love, the soul of radiant light who can act as a St. George (or St. Margaret) in its own right. (See figure 3, page 10, and plate 1, page 43.)

Every human being can learn how to become a St. George. First we need to become sufficiently virgin or pure in love. Then, by actively shining our love or heart-light out to others, we can help to unlock and release their potential. Likewise we can shine our light onto nature, releasing the imprisoned energies of the Earth. In taking this role, we not only help the planet to evolve toward a sphere of light and beauty, but at the same time help ourselves to evolve toward an expression of our full potential.

The evolution and perfection of the soul does not take place overnight. It is achieved through right effort and goodwill (*i.e.* strife and friendship), helped by a process of life that takes place within the life form. The process is associated with time, and the form with space. The process is the complement (or polarity) to the form, just as time is the complement (or polarity) to space. The process inspires the form, and the form enables the process to express itself.

ST. GEORGE AND THE DRAGON

St. George, the shining Rose Cross knight and "Spear-shaker," was called upon by a king and his people to rescue them from distress. Not only was a mighty dragon laying waste their land each year, but it was devouring their children. The beautiful and much-loved daughter of the king and queen had been the latest victim of this fearful creature.

Figure 3. St. George and the Dragon.
The myth of St. George and the Dragon is an allegory of the human soul, awakened from the sleep of ignorance by spiritual love so that it can be transformed into a fully self-conscious form of light and beauty.

St. George, having been entreated by the king and queen and all the people, went to the mouth of the cave where the dragon lay asleep in the dark depths of the rock. Blowing his horn and shining light into the cave to awaken the dragon, St. George managed to draw the great creature out of its lair. The disgruntled dragon, catching sight of the disturber of its sleep, immediately attacked the knight, and a great battle took place.

Eventually St. George overcame the dragon, piercing it with his lance and mortally wounding it. As the dragon died, its belly burst open and out stepped the princess, released from her dark prison. Embracing her savior, she rode off with him to her parents.

The king and queen and all the people rejoiced at their delivery and to see the princess safe. With the consent of his wife and daughter, the king offered the hand of the princess to the knight in gratitude. Then, shortly afterward, amid grand celebrations, the princess and St. George were married. In the course of time they inherited the now peaceful and prosperous kingdom, and a child of great beauty and wisdom was born to them.

Time and the Process of Life

*The three foundations of holiness and illumination from
God are:
To love truth, to understand truth, and to serve truth.*
—LLYWELN SION, DRUIDIC WISDOM

TIME CYCLES

Life manifests within an endless series of time cycles. The end of one
cycle is the beginning of the next, and within every cycle a process of
life takes place, each with recognizable stages. These stages are four in
number—a trinity of three stages issuing from an initial one. All cycles
of time have these four major stages or quarters. In our lives the most
obvious examples are the daily twenty-four hour cycle, with its natural
division into night, morning, noon, and evening, and the annual cycle
with its four seasons. Out of winter come spring, summer, and autumn,
and out of the night come morning, noon, and evening.

THE NATURE CYCLE

The year is a solar cycle in which the Earth makes one complete circuit
of the Sun. Each of its four seasons has its own particular purpose.

Winter is primarily the season of rest and preparation for renewed
life, when the seed lies dormant in the ground. It is also the time of ger-
mination, the birth or first beginnings of a new expression of life. With

the dawning of spring, buds and green shoots burst from the darkness of the mother plant or earth into the light of day, to come into full flowering in the summer. With autumn comes the fruit, and the harvest: and within each fruit lie the seeds of new growth, of new life, to be sown into the ground with the coming of the next winter. Each year begins with birth and ends with death, and out of that death is born the next new year, all in perfect order. Life itself never ceases, and death, like birth, is simply a stage in each life cycle.

In our own lives, as in nature, the purpose of every seed—every new impulse and intention—is to grow into a plant that produces fruit. Ultimately the fruit dies so that the seed it contains can be released into the ground, to bring more life—and often to bring it more abundantly, for one seed can produce a plant with many fruits, and each fruit may contain many seeds.

In modern urban living we tend to be cut off from these natural cycles, and may feel a sense of resistance to changes in the seasons, let alone the processes of aging and dying. But, by becoming attuned to life's purpose and process, we can help ourselves to live consciously in harmony with this natural progression, and without fear. (See figure 4, page 13.)

THE EIGHT SOLAR FESTIVALS

Within each cycle of time there are eight major power-points or chakras in time. In the annual cycle these are known as the eight Solar Festivals. We can learn to observe these and work with them, to our great advantage. (See table 1, page 14.)

Four of the power points occur at the midpoints of the seasons, when the seasonal energy is at its height. The other four power points occur at the cusps of the seasons, where one season turns into the next. These eight power points are the most critical times in the life cycle. At these times ancient peoples, including our Celtic ancestors, held three-day festivals known as Solar or Fire Festivals. Although today they have lost most of their original significance, they are still to be found within the Christian calendar (see figure 5, page 15.)

The midpoint of each season is clearly delineated by the position of the Sun in relation to the Earth. Hence Midwinter and Midsummer are marked by the solstices, the longest and the shortest nights of the year. Midspring and Midautumn are marked by the equinoxes, when the Sun rises due east and sets due west on a level horizon, and the twenty-four hours are divided equally between day and night.

*Figure 4. The Wheel of Life. (Sun-wheel forming one of the twelve wheels
of Vishnu's solar chariot, carved on the 13th century Hindu temple of
Vishnu-Surya at Konarak in Orissa, India).*

In all the great world traditions, the cycle of time is depicted as an eight-spoked
wheel. In different cultures it is called the Wheel of Life, the Wheel of Karma,
the Wheel of Birth and Death, the Wheel of Fortune, the Wheel of Fate, and the
Wheel of Destiny. In some countries it is known as the Medicine Wheel. Mastering it brings health, happiness, and fulfillment to the individual, and ultimately to whole communities and the world itself. The wheel symbolizes every
cycle of life, great and small, in which we are all involved.

The other four great festivals come at the cusps of the seasons. These
are less clearly marked by the position of the Sun, but they can be sensed
or even observed in nature. For instance, the beginning of summer is
marked by the sudden and dramatic leafing and blossoming of the majority of deciduous trees. In Britain and other parts of northern Europe
this phenomenon, associated with the beginning of May, is represented
by the blossoming May tree. The Celts sometimes celebrated these
occasions at the Full Moon nearest to the cusp, thus marrying the fiery
solar cycle to the watery lunar cycle four times a year. In our modern

Table 1. The Eight Solar Festivals (Celtic and Christian).

Dec. 22–25	Winter Solstice Midwinter	*Geerah* Christmas	Festival of Birth and Rebirth
Feb. 2	1st Quarterday Winter/Spring cusp	*Imbolc* Candlemas	Festival of Dedication
March 21	Spring Equinox Midspring	*Antharoc* Lady Day	Festival of Promise
May 1	2nd Quarterday Spring/Summer cusp	*Beltain* May Day	Festival of Unification
June 21–24	Summer Solstice Midsummer	*Saura* Midsummer's Day	Festival of Joy
Aug. 8	3rd Quarterday Summer/Autumn cusp	*Lugnasadh* First Fruits	Festival of Transformation
Sept. 22–24	Autumn Equinox Midautumn	*Law Aila Miheel* Harvest Festival	Festival of Consummation
Nov. 1	4th Quarterday Autumn/Winter cusp	*Samhain* All Hallows Day	Festival of Death and Peace

calendar, the cusps are sometimes known as the Quarterday Festivals, dividing the year into its four quarters or seasons.

In Celtic and pre-Celtic times the correct dates were also found through the use of great alignments or ley-lines (light-lines) laid across the landscape, marked by sacred mounds, stones, or other features, and aligned to the rising (or setting) Sun on the days of the Solar Festivals. One of the best known of these ancient alignments is the St. Michael-Mary line which stretches for hundreds of miles across southern England, from St. Michael's Mount in Cornwall to Bury St. Edmunds in East Anglia. The alignment marks the rising Sun on May Day, or Beltain, and also indicates the other Quarterdays.

The Celts marked the eight festivals with three-day celebrations or holy-days (holidays) known as fire festivals, at which they lit bonfires ("good fires") representing the Sun and its light, on special sites or power points in the landscape.

On these festival days the whole community, led by their elders, would process to the power points. These processions were a way of

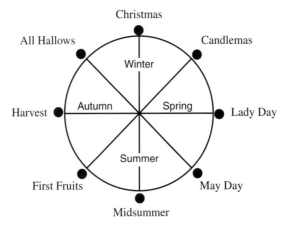

Figure 5. The Nature Cycle and the Eight Solar Festivals.
The four quarters or seasons are delineated by a St. Andrew's Cross, or Saltire, marking the Quarterday festivals. The midpoints of the seasons are defined by a Rose Cross, or St. George's Cross.

working with the Earth energies and life forces of the landscape, helping them to flow in the right ways and to keep the environment healthy and vitalized.

In this way, by drawing up the Earth energies to unite with the spiritual energies from the cosmos, which pierce the power points like spears of light, our ancestors cooperated with the natural cycles to mediate between Heaven and Earth. They helped the spiritual and Earth energies blend together, to create light and joy, treating the landscape itself as sacred, as a temple; and when temples are looked after and function properly, the whole land tends to become more fertile, the weather more balanced, and the atmosphere or ambience more vitalized and life-enhancing. Celebrations like these carried out in the right places help to make people healthier and happier.

Today there is a reviving awareness of the need to work with the seasons and with sacred places. Celebrating the major power points in time greatly enhances the development of every individual, and of society as a whole, and today it is exciting to see that there are an increasing number of groups who gather to celebrate them at special places.

Not only are these festivals good for the community and the Earth, they are also extremely vitalizing and a regular boost to the labor of everyday life. Psychologically and physically it is immensely helpful and rejuvenating to have a short holiday every six weeks, which includes a celebration with a meaning and purpose. It is good psychology, and brings an added meaning and enjoyment to our lives.

Individuals can tune in to these natural power points in time simply by being aware of them and their meaning. We can enhance them (and thus our lives) by marking them with a specific meditation or prayer, or by engaging in an appropriate activity. This can also be done every day, using the power points of each daily cycle (i.e., the "magic hours" of 3:00, 6:00, 9:00 and 12:00).

Attuning ourselves to the rhythms of time, we can support our own and our planet's evolution. Rhythm is the driving power of the creative life force, known in the East as Shiva's drum, the heartbeat of the Universe. By following the rhythms of nature, we can consistently give regular impulses of energy and love-light to the world and to our own lives, at the appropriate times.

THE HUMAN CYCLE:
IMPULSE–DESIRE–THOUGHT–ACTION

In human life, the cycle that repeats itself over and over again is that of impulse-desire-thought-action. Underlying every human action is some kind of thought, whether conscious or subconscious, and underlying every thought is a desire. The desire proceeds from some kind of initial impulse, either internal or external.

Before doing anything we have first to want to do it. That desire is our energizing force—our motivation, or e-motion. Emotion is not identical with feelings, which comprise our sensitivity and reactions to emotion. Emotion, or desire, is our motivating force—our will and energy. Every desire or emotion leads to a thought, in which we perceive what we want and plan our action. Finally, we put the thought into action. These three phases of desire, thought, and action express the trinity, the fundamental law of life. If we add to the three the originating impulse we have four stages:

1. The beginning or first impulse, out of which comes
2. Desire or emotion, followed by
3. Thought or perception, followed by
4. Material manifestation or action.

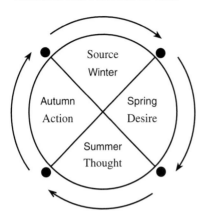

Figure 6. Annual Cycle/Human Cycle.

This cycle repeats itself constantly, from the most mundane actions to the most important. If you consider your life, you will see that whatever you do, from making a cup of tea to embarking on a career, or following a spiritual path, you will inevitably follow these four steps.

This human cycle corresponds beautifully with the cycle of the seasons. From the depth of our being springs a previously dormant desire; this flowers into a thought and comes to fruition as an action. Thus, we have our winter (source), spring (desire), summer (thought) and autumn (action) continuously repeated throughout our lives, sometimes in long time-cycles, sometimes in short ones. (See figure 6, above.)

THE FOUR ELEMENTS

The four seasons, or four stages of the life process, are related to the four alchemical elements, *earth, water, air,* and *fire.* The *earth* refers to the beginning stage, the season of winter and the first impulse born in the darkness of matter. Spring, and the emotions, are symbolized by *water.* Summertime, and thoughts, are related to *air;* and autumn, the time of action, is symbolized by *fire.*

Alchemy is the chemistry of Al, the All (i.e., Universal Being or Existence). Alchemists are those who observe life carefully, and work with its laws, with the aim of producing harmony, beauty, knowledge of truth, and joy. The alchemical elements are derived from a careful observation of nature, and form a symbolic language for understanding all things physical and metaphysical.

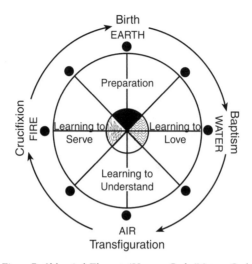

Figure 7. Alchemical Elements/Human Cycle/Nature Cycle.

For instance, a simple and clear example of the four alchemical elements and their sequence is contained in a lighted candle. Under the influence of heat, carefully applied, the cold hard wax (*earth*) of the candle melts to form a liquid (*water*). The liquid then vaporizes and the vapor (*air*) subsequently bursts into flame (*fire*). Within the flame, and shining from it, is light, the *quintessence*.

The analogy of the alchemical elements, and of nature in its seasonal changes, to the human life process forms a language used by our great poets and initiates down the ages. Fairy tales, stories of the hero's quest, the allegories and mysteries of initiation, the Shakespeare plays, the sacred Scriptures, all use the same basic symbolic language. (See figure 7, above.)

PERFECTING THE CYCLE

When, in any cycle, the four stages of the human life process are taken to their highest possible expression, the initial impulse will be good, desire becomes loving, thought becomes understanding, and action becomes service. This results in a knowledge of truth and a joy in what has been achieved. At the start, however, in the usually imperfect conditions of everyday life, these four stages are: 1) a mundane impulse; 2) ordinary desire (or imperfect love); 3) ordinary thought (or imperfect understanding); 4) ordinary action and reaction (or imperfect service). At their worst, the impulses, desires, thoughts, and actions of some people are gross or even perverse. We repeat this fundamental cycle (of impulse-desire-thought-action) over and over again throughout our lives, often making one mistake after another. How then can we move from imperfection to perfection?

We can, in fact, gradually perfect each cycle by becoming more consciously aware of what we are doing and why, and of the results of our actions, and then making an effort to do better next time. Whenever an action is complete, that particular cycle comes to an end, and there follows a moment of waiting and resting. This can be a time of recuperation. Most important of all, it is a period in which we can recall the experience and gain knowledge from it.

Every time we perform an action and remember it, we gain knowledge from that particular experience. Such knowledge is real, experiential knowledge, not just intellectual knowledge. It is not until we have lived through an experience that we really know what it means to us.

So, at the end of a complete cycle of impulse, desire, thought, and action, the certain knowledge based upon our achievement will feed in to the next impulse. This knowledge is the seed from which will spring the next desire, and the next thought and action. By using our knowledge and awareness we can grow better at living and learn to avoid repeating our mistakes, at the same time gaining more knowledge, as one cycle is followed by another and then another. As we benefit from our knowledge, the evolutionary process, itself, becomes speeded up.

The more consciously we repeat this cycle, the more we can learn from the mistakes or successes of the previous one. And the more we ally good intentions to our activities, the more are we able to transform the imperfect cycle of impulse-desire-thought-action into the perfect cycle of inspiration-loving-understanding-service. In this perfected cycle the divine nature of love becomes fully manifest.

THE PATH OF INITIATION

When we set out deliberately to live our lives as perfectly as possible, we can be said to enter on the path of initiation. We take this path when,

each time we begin a new cycle, we consciously and deliberately dedicate the new desire to be the very best we are capable of, together with
the thoughts and actions proceeding from the desire. Thus we begin the
process of mastering life.

In each cycle of initiation, there is first a period of preparation, a time
of assimilating and learning from the results of the previous cycle while
waiting for the impulse of the new cycle to be born. This is the winter
period. What is known as the first degree of initiation is the spring
period—learning to love. The second degree is the summer period—
learning to understand. The third degree is the autumn period—
learning to serve.

Christianity refers to these three degrees of initiation as faith, hope,
and charity. Faith, which is our ability to love positively and creatively,
and be receptive to love, is the foundation; hope, which is our vision and
understanding of love, is the mediator; and charity, which is our love and
understanding put into action as service, is the fruit and crown of the
cycle, and the greatest of the three because it fulfils the purpose of the
other degrees.

The allegorical or mystery names given to these degrees of initiation,
including the initial period of preparation, are: 1) birth (in the cave); 2)
baptism (by water); 3) transfiguration (high in the air on the mountain
top); and 4) crucifixion (on the fiery cross of service). The final result—
the *quintessence* of the initiatic cycle—is resurrection (or revelation),
which is an inestimable joy and knowledge of truth, which lights up the
whole soul and body, and bestows certain powers or abilities. This itself
is a gateway that leads to even further degrees of attainment.

The keys to doing this well lie in the power points in time, particularly the moments when each stage ends and the next stage begins.

THE FOUR KEYS—DEDICATION,
TESTING, OFFERING, AND THANKSGIVING

There are four key moments in each cycle of life. These correspond to
the four Quarterdays, and they are probably the most important of the
power points in time in our lives. Forming the Saltire Cross in the emblem of the Wheel of Life, they are symbolized by the Keys of St. Peter.
These four power points also correspond to the four Cherubim who
guard the gates of Paradise.

The word Paradise comes from a Hebrew word represented by the
letters *PRDS*, which are associated with the four quarters of the wheel

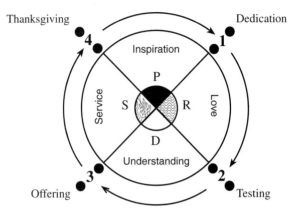

Figure 8. The Gates of Paradise.

of life: *P*—winter/*earth*; *R*—spring/*water*, *D*—summer/*air*, *S*—autumn/ *fire*. They represent the major stages of initiation: inspiration–love–understanding–service. To enter Paradise we have to go through each of the gates, passing each cherubic gatekeeper by carrying out each stage of initiation consciously and perfectly. (See figure 8, above.)

Key 1—Dedication (Imbolc/Candlemas)

The first gate comes after the "winter" period of preparation, at the time when we first become aware of a desire. This is the moment to dedicate the desire. Our desire is our will or motive, which motivates us to think and act in a certain way. The key to open this gate to Paradise is to consciously and deliberately make our will the will of God, of Love. This ensures that our desire develops as a loving, caring, life-giving emotion. The dedication is our password, and the Cherub opens this first gate to Paradise when we sound the note of love.

A vital part of any cycle is our will or intention at the start. We can choose consciously and deliberately to dedicate each new desire (which leads to a new thought and action) to be the very best we are capable of—whether it is an everyday activity or a major, life-changing project.

Besides dedicating our own individual desires, it is also good for groups or communities to do the same. Nowadays many groups which meet for spiritual or other purposes (even business meetings) will dedicate their meeting by pausing for a moment's silence before they begin. We can equally well make our dedication on our own.

Dedication does not have to involve an elaborate ritual. It can be the simple act of pausing before embarking on a new activity, or a new day, and mentally stating our intention that this activity, or this day, will be dedicated to the highest good. The dedication helps our desire, and everything else that arises from it, to be a good, wise and helpful one.

In the annual cycle Imbolc (Candlemas) is the time of dedication, when we make (or reiterate) our new year vow.

Key 2—Testing (Beltain/May Day)

The stage of desire or emotion, when developed as a true lovingness, creative and receptive, makes us more sensitive and caring to others and our environment. Since emotion is an energy, which vibrates within and all around us, emotion speaks to our mind as an inner voice. Our sensitive awareness of, and listening to, this voice constitutes our intuition. Our vision is developed from this intuition, in the "eye" (or imagination) of our mind. The true voice, which creates the true idea or vision, is the voice of love. This is what is tested at this second gate—whether it be love or no. Is it peaceful? Is it good? Is it helpful? Will it be useful and good to others?

At this power point, or gate, in the time cycle, the inner voice is speaking strongly to the mind and our mind wants to think about it. This is the moment when the vision or idea is first formed. Once our mind has its vision or idea, it has something concrete to think about. Some people are better than others in forming a clear vision; but, however we do it, concurrent with the forming of the vision comes a second voice—the voice of the Tester. This inner voice always challenges the first voice. Some people call it the voice of conscience. It is the second Cherub or Gatekeeper, whose purpose is to test the idea that has arisen from our desire, and to set our mind thinking about it. It also helps to make the vision clearer.

The festival marking this power point in time is known as Unification, because several sequential unions or "marriages" take place within us at this time—the marriage of heart with mind, of intuition with intellect, and of imagination with reason. In the annual cycle, Beltain (May Day) used to be the popular and customary time of marriage, with the bride wearing May blossoms in her hair.

Key 3—Offering (Lugnasadh/First Fruits)

Despite good intentions, many mistakes are made in life because people rush quickly from an idea into action without double checking whether it really is a good idea and whether they have understood it correctly and sufficiently. At the third gate, which comes at the climax of the thinking stage, we need to pause, double check, and offer our developed idea or plan of action to our highest self—to divine Love; thus the original dedication becomes an offering.

When we truly make the offering, asking inwardly whether or not it is a good plan, we will receive very clear feedback as to whether or not to go ahead with the action. If the answer is no, it is not a good plan, then we have the chance to think some more or start again. But if we receive confirmation from our highest self (or the Cherub of this gate) that the plan is good, then this bestows a kind of inner authority, giving us extra courage and empowerment. Now we can bring our idea down to earth by putting it into action, with full courage and power.

This festival in the annual cycle is referred to as Transformation, for it is the time when the flowers transform into fruit, and our ideas into action.

Key 4—Thanksgiving and Remembrance (Samhain/All Hallows)

At this final key moment in the cycle we have completed our activity. Now is the time to give thanks and look back on our achievement, remembering it. If we have done well, it will make us feel happy, giving us joy and knowledge of what really is good and worthwhile. If we have not succeeded as well as we had hoped, at least we will have gained the knowledge to do better next time. Together, thanksgiving and remembrance bring real knowledge.

In the annual cycle this power point in time is known as Peace. It is also the moment of death, when the activity has finished, the task completed. This is, or should be, a time of peace. Peace is associated with rest and refreshment, and also with joy and illumination. At Samhain (All Hallows) we remember and give thanks to all those good souls who have helped us and the world, and who have found their peace. In the original celebration of Samhain the guy, representing our old self who has served well, is placed on the bonfire so that it might be consumed in fire, so releasing its light to bless the community and the land.

If we have done well, we will hear the Cherub of this gate saying: "Well done, thou good and faithful servant." And this last gate will then be opened into the state of Paradise, the state of illumined joy and peace.

Going through the Gates

Anything we do, whether a mundane task or a complex ceremony, has its own complete cycle. Every cycle has its time of preparation, its time to let love and intuition develop, its time to formulate the idea and plan of action, then its time of action, with the gates between each stage and at the end.

However, for us to live each and every cycle well, recognizing each stage and each gateway, is difficult, so it is easier to work consciously at first with the bigger cycles: for instance, the yearly cycle with its major festivals, or any cycle involving a major project in our lives. With practice, we can gradually arrive at a recognition of the smaller and seemingly less important cycles, and work to perfect them as well.

Such work, or effort, is one that will make us a yogi or saint—someone who has found conscious and joyful union, or at-one-ness, with Universal Love, Universal Life.

THE MYTHOLOGICAL CYCLE OF THE SOLAR FESTIVALS

Because the cycle of the year relates to the human cycle of initiation, the ancient practice of celebrating the Solar Festivals attached an allegorical story of the human soul to the nature cycle. In this way people throughout the world were taught in the past, and still can be taught today, how the human cycle goes hand in hand with and is analogous to the nature cycle. The stories used were the allegorical stories of the initiate or hero, from the hero's birth to his death. Following the hero's death there was always his resurrection or rebirth, just as the sunlight, time, and nature's virility, appear to be reborn every year. The traditional hero was, therefore, always associated with these three things—light, time, and fertility; and, as all three come from the Sun, the hero was associated with the Sun, as a sun-god.

Associating the human soul with the Sun, as well as with light, time, and fertility, is not just an allegorical fiction, but a profound truth. All life on our planet depends on the Sun. The Earth was born from the Sun, and is held in and nourished by the Sun's light, including the invisible life-force (Sanskrit, *prana*) of its electro-magnetic energy field. The sunlight provides warmth and light and life: through photosynthesis, for instance, plant life converts the Sun's light into digestible energy forms for our own bodies and other creatures, as well as for itself. Light is, in fact, a substance as well as an energy, which we eat in a modified form and build into our bodies.

As for the *prana* of the sunlight, this reaches us as a "breath" or solar wind—an invisible energy which waxes and wanes, and which provides the dynamism and force of all phenomenal life on our planet. The rhythm and cycles of this "breath" are governed by the polar and equatorial rotations of the Sun's two magnetic fields, of which the sun-spot cycle is a phenomenal manifestation. All the time we breathe and absorb this *prana,* and are affected by its nature.

Phenomenal life on this planet is completely dependant upon and influenced by the light, the energy, and the behavioral patterns of the Sun, the Earth's parent. In addition, the Sun's life and behavior is, itself, affected and modified by the movement of the planets around it (and to some extent, as far as we know, by its relationship to other stars)— the knowledge and experience of which lies behind the science of astrology, for anything that affects the Sun in turn affects us *via* the Sun.

Both the *prana* (energy) and substance of sunlight are material realities, as two poles of material existence. But complementing this is the spiritual Sun and its light—the Sun behind the Sun, which great traditions refer to as the Sun of Righteousness and Light of Wisdom.

The word "soul" is derived from the name of the Sun—*Sol.* The human soul comes from the Sun, and belongs to the Sun. Its nature is light, the same nature as that of the Sun, its parent and source. The human body (in which the soul dwells), like that of the Earth, is made out of the material substance of the Sun—a substance which has become "hardened,"dark and gross, but in which the soul finds experience of both light and dark, and hence gains both strength and a knowledge of truth.

The great heroes or sun-gods are all, for this reason, personifications of the Sun (*e.g.* Brahma, Vishnu and Shiva of the Hindus, Osiris and Horus of the Egyptians, Bel or Bal of the Chaldeans, Adonai of the Phoenicians, Adonis, Apollo and Bacchus of the Greeks, Mithras of the Persians and Romans, Arthur, Hu and Bal of the Celts, the Messiah of the Hebrews and Jesus of the Christians).

Every hero or sun-god is associated with a mother, a virgin, who is the "light-bearer" and the mother of the light, the sun-god. Not only does the mother relate to the Sun, itself, parent of the human soul, but also to the outer form which contains and gives birth to the perfect soul or light. This outer form is both material and psychological, being our personality as distinct from our soul. The personality is the dragon of myth which, when purified, becomes transformed into the virgin. The allegories connected with the annual cycle thus contain stories about the virgin mother as well as the sun-god or hero. The story of each annual cycle therefore, with its festivals, typically shows three evolutionary levels of manifestation—the nature cycle (parodying the dragon cycle), the virgin cycle and the sun-god cycle.

Festival of Birth and Rebirth (Christmas)

On the day immediately following the midwinter Solstice, the sun-god or hero is born in a cave, deep in the Earth, surrounded by the creatures of the zodiac. His mother is a virgin, one who is pure in love, understanding, and service. Helping her is a young girl, who prepares herself and dreams of the future.

In nature the seed, buried in the ground, germinates; and in our hearts the light of love is rekindled, reborn for another cycle of manifestation. We light fires in the hearth, the heart of the house, give presents of love and joy, and decorate our rooms with red-berried holly, white-berried mistletoe and evergreen laurel, symbolic of the trinity and the ever-livingness of nature. The evergreen fir stands proud as the tree of life, hung with apples and lights, fruits of knowledge and life, and decorated with bright ribbons signifying the beauty of nature inherent in all things. In the twelve days which follow (the Twelve Days of Christmas), the cycle of the whole year is enacted out in miniature, as a promise or seed for the future, each day representing a sign of the zodiac and culminating with Epiphany.

Festival of Dedication (Candlemas)

The young maiden emerges from the underworld of winter, undergoes purification in the fresh waters of the sacred spring, and dedicates herself and her life to the expression of love. The mother takes her young son to the temple, where the sun-god is offered and his life dedicated to the good of all, while she purifies and dedicates herself anew.

In nature the ice and snow melt, the streams rush from the ground, water bathes the Earth, the first snowdrops appear and lambs start to be born. All nature begins to come alive with a vital energy, and with a hint of promise in the atmosphere. We drink the pure water from the sacred

well, light candles and lanterns in the sacred places, and make our vows
for the year.

Festival of Promise (Ladyday)

At midspring the lovers meet and a love-troth is made. The maiden
is fertilized with the seed of love; a promise is given of her future
child. The heroes sail the seas, tempest-tossed, braving and stilling the
storms.

Nature vibrates with life; buds are sprouting everywhere. We become
filled with love, sexual and romantic, dreaming dreams with rose-colored
glasses, filled with energy and an intuitive promise of the future, when
all things feel possible.

Festival of Unification (Mayday)

After final rites of purification in the bridal bath, the lovers walk between the twin bonfires and marry in the sacred circle. The young hero,
after the baptism is over, is drawn out of the water by the hierophant.
He hears the inner voice giving him his spiritual name and purpose, and
sees the vision of the light, the wisdom, that shines from his own heart
and the heart of nature. Immediately he is tested, to see if he under-
stands what he hears and sees, and if he can truly overcome the desires
which give him tempting thoughts. He is accepted into the universal
brotherhood of light and taught the holy wisdom.

Nature explodes with blossom, drinking in and marrying with the
sunlight. All is ablaze with color. We bathe our bodies and faces in the
May dew; then, decked with garlands of flowers we dance together
around the maypole, the flowering tree of life, learning how to weave
our lives together in a beautiful, exciting, and meaningful way.

Festival of Joy (Midsummer)

The sun-god presides at the "round table" gathering of heroes, with the
grail in their midst. With great rejoicing the virgin is perceived to be
bearing the child of light in her womb. The vision of truth is seen and
understood.

Nature rejoices in the bright color and sunlight of Midsummer.
Fields of wheat and barley grow strong. Chains of bonfires are lit on
high places, stretching far across the countryside. Midsummer gatherings
take place, and couples, hand in hand, jump the fires in celebration of
the light and in anticipation of the coming harvest.

Festival of Transformation (First Fruits, Transfiguration)

The sun-god leads his disciples up to the summit of the high mountain, where their consciousness is raised and they offer their vision to the highest good. Transfigured with light, the sun-god then leads them down the mountain and into the valleys, to heal the sick, to help the poor and needy, and to free the land from tyranny. The pregnant mother, feeling the second life beating strongly within her, gives thanks.

The first fruits appear in nature. In the fields the first sheaves of ripe wheat and barley are cut, and the grain made into bread. The first bread and fruits are offered to God, and given to the poor and hungry. Flaming wheels are rolled down hillsides, representing the descent of Midsummer light into the autumn of the year, and of wisdom and compassion coming into the world in an act of service.

Festival of Consummation (Harvest)

The sun-god leads the heroes in procession of thanksgiving; tyranny is defeated, the land is healed and the people prosperous. With the whole community helping, the main harvest is gathered in, and a harvest thanksgiving and celebration feast enjoyed.

Festival of Peace (All Hallows)

The sun-god is recognized and declared Son and heir, lord of all. At the last feast of friendship and thanksgiving he completes the offering of himself, his life and light, for the good of all. He shares his grail of knowledge. His earthly form dies, transmuted into light. The round table of his disciples is dissolved. A peace ensues as the land and people rest. The virgin prepares to give birth to a new expression of light.

In the fields the final sheaves are threshed, the grain is made into bread, or sown into the ground ready for the new cycle. The chaff and straw is burned, and dug back into the earth. The autumn leaves fall from the trees; the sap returns back to the roots. Fires are lit in celebration and thanksgiving to the old year, and on them is burned the "guy," a symbolic representation of the hero who has done his work and is now ready for his old form to die, to be transmuted into light in the fire of peace. A feast of remembrance is held, to remember and give thanks to the great teachers and wise ones of all ages, to the saints and holy people, and to all souls everywhere.

SECONDARY RHYTHMS

The four seasons and their eight power points, marked by the Solar Festivals, constitute the major life rhythm for our planet. Added to this, and taking place within this major life cycle, are various secondary rhythms of great importance to our lives.

The Twelve Months

In the annual time-cycle there are the four seasons and the eight power points; but, just as all life is basically a trinity, so each season or quarter is itself a trinity. This combines to manifest twelve distinct sections of the time cycle or Wheel of Life, which the zodiac of twelve celestial "creatures" represents, each creature being signified by a constellation of stars through which the Sun progresses in its apparent movement about the Earth (as seen from the Earth).

Over this zodiacal Round Table the sun-god presides, represented either as the Sun in the center of its solar system and universe, or as the Sun encircling the Earth, progressing along the ecliptic or Sun's path and passing through each of the zodiacal constellations in turn. The latter represents the soul on its evolutionary journey, experiencing the cycle of life and encountering the eight power points with their four great gates of initiation. As it does this, the soul also passes through the

Table 2. The Zodiac Divisions of the Year.

Zodiacal Sign	Approx. Time Period
Capricorn, the Goat	December 21–January 19
Aquarius, the Water-Bearer	January 20–February 17
Pisces, the Fishes	February 18–March 19
Aries, the Ram	March 20–April 19
Taurus, the Bull (Ox)	April 20–May 20
Gemini, the Twins	May 21–June 20
Cancer, the Crab	June 21–July 22
Leo, the Lion	July 23–August 22
Virgo, the Virgin	August 23–September 22
Libra, the Scales	September 23–October 22
Scorpio, the Scorpion (Eagle)	October 23–November 21
Sagittarius, the Archer	November 22–December 20

twelve phases of life represented by the twelve signs, constellations and creatures of the zodiac.

These twelve time periods constitute the twelve astrological months of the year, each of approximately 30 days, and each with its own energy, consciousness, and purpose which have a corresponding effect on us. The stories of the twelve Knights of the Round Table who each have a task to perform, and of the Grail Knight who attains the Grail when he has overcome twelve challenges, and the twelve labors of Hercules, all refer to our experience of the time cycle in this way. The traditional stories provide us with insights into what to expect and how to cope with the challenges of life. (See table 2, page 29.)

The astrological signs of the zodiac are an ideal, representing an archetype or governing "seed" from which all variations proceed. The actual astronomical truth is the zodiac of constellations slowly moves in an apparent circle around the Earth, such that their relationship to sunrise at the different times of the year changes over a long period of time. This phenomenon is known as the precession of the equinoxes and is due to the "wobble" of the Earth's axis. It produces an effect such that, for instance, the cusp of Aries-Pisces, known as the Point of Aries, which marked the position of the rising Sun at the Spring Equinox approximately 2,000 years ago, has gradually moved so that it now marks the rising Sun in April, one month later. The rising Sun at the Spring Equinox now appears at the cusp of Pisces-Aquarius. For this reason, it is said that we are on the point of entering the Age of Aquarius, each Age being marked by the position in the zodiac of the rising Sun at the Spring Equinox.

In addition, the actual sizes of the zodiacal constellations vary, so that, astronomically speaking, the time periods of some Ages are different

Figure 9. The Zodiac
(The Solar Circle of Creatures).
The Sun, accompanied by its planets, passes annually through the twelve "creatures"— the constellations and signs of the zodiac. Its journey is representative of our own journey in life.

from others, and the corresponding divisions of the zodiac are not all the same, some being larger than others. But both viewpoints (the astronomical and the astrological) have validity, and both should always be taken into account by us, as the ancient sages always did. Myth incorporates the two—the fixed archetype and the fluid phenomenal reality—as creative polarities to each other. (See figure 9, page 30.)

The Solar Wind

Added to the twelvefold rhythm is another rhythm, this time derived from the Sun's "breath," which affects us intimately. The Sun continually "breathes" its energy upon us, bathing the world in its *prana* or breath. This breath, referred to by modern scientists as the solar wind, has its own cycle and rhythm, which is likened to an inbreath and an outbreath. The solar wind takes approximately forty-eight hours to reach the Earth and, because of the differential rotation of the two magnetic fields of the Sun and the rotation of the Earth about the Sun, the combined effect is that the solar wind bathes the Earth with alternating polarity, with the switch in polarity occurring every seven days, like an "outbreath" and an "inbreath." The division of the year into seven-day weeks is in recognition of this rhythmic flow of the Sun's energy, as also is the allegorical description of the creation of the world in seven days by the "breath of God," the breath of Love.

Our year, marking one revolution of the Earth around the Sun, is composed of approximately 365 days. In this time there are fifty-two weeks, thirteen to each season, plus one extra day. From this comes the term, "a year and a day." The year in this context refers to a cycle of fifty-two weeks or twenty-six complete solar breaths. The four-week, 28-day period of two complete solar breaths is counted as one month in the Druidic 13-month calendar. The extra day is known as "the Day out of Time," which the Druids used to celebrate annually at the Winter Solstice as Mistletoe Day, lying between the old year and the new, and belonging to neither. The standard pack of playing cards, containing fifty-two cards in four sets, plus a Joker, was designed to represent this solar cycle: playing with cards being a parody of the game of life.

The Joker signifies Saturn or Pan, the Spirit of Time and of Nature, who rules over the Christmas period as the Christmas Jester or Lord of Misrule. Traditionally he is said to turn things upside down, for he turns death into rebirth. Various cultures have acted this out for millennia in their Midwinter festivities, appointing a Lord of Misrule to rule over their society during the Christmas period, with various customs reversed plus a lot of jesting and good humor. During this time, for instance, in Rome and elsewhere, slaves became "freemen," crimes were pardoned, masters became "servants," and the servants "masters." The remnants of this custom still exist today, in Germany for example, in the Carnival Prince.

In essence, the Spirit of Time represents the spiritual Sun, source of our being. He is the Alpha and Omega, the beginning and the end of the cycle of manifestation. The six-pointed Blazing Star or Christ Star is traditionally the symbol of this—the star which announces the new birth of light in the winter cave of the new cycle—the star seen by the Magi, the wise ones.

In effect though, despite the symbolism associated with Midwinter, the "Day out of Time" is a moveable feast, because the flow and rhythm of the solar wind does not stop for the extra day in the year. What actually happens is that the 52-week annual cycle of the solar wind creates an apparent retrograde effect of the "extra day" as the years go by. That is to say, the extra day moves backward in the calendar, occurring, for instance, on December 23rd in one year, but on December 22nd the next, and December 21st the year after that. Except during leap years the extra day moves back a day in the calendar each year: in a leap year it moves back two days. In approximately 270 years it will have completed a whole retrograde cycle and will occur on December 24th, ready to begin a new revolution. (See figure 10, below.)

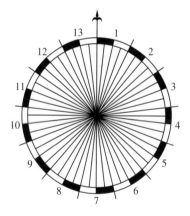

Figure 10. The Solar Wind Cycle (52 weeks, 13 months, 26 breaths).

The Jester: Because the extra "day-out-of-time" can be seen as moving around the circle of the calendar, as an alternative to being perceived as stationary at the Midwinter point, in card games the Jester can be treated as a "wild card": that is to say, it can be placed anywhere in the circle and represent any one of the 52 cards or weeks of the year.

The Phoenix Cycle

The 270 years is significant, for this constitutes one eighth of an astrological Age. An astrological Age is one-twelfth of a so-called Phoenix Cycle or Great Age, sometimes called a Sidereal Year, caused by the wobble of the Earth's axis, which makes the celestial north pole of the planet (*i.e.* the axis of the planet projected up into the northern sky) move in a circle. This circle is traced out by the celestial north pole around the occult north pole, center of the ecliptic and the zodiac. The

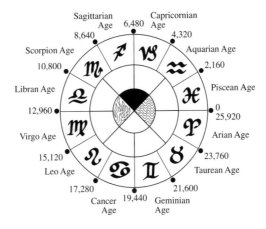

Figure 11. The Phoenix Cycle.

The Phoenix Cycle is approximately a 26,000 year cycle—a Great Age consisting of Twelve Ages, each of approximately 2,160 years. The Phoenix is a symbol of the perpetual creation, destruction and transmutation—or of the birth, death, and resurrection—of the cosmos, including all that lives within the cosmos. The symbolism of the phoenix is derived from that of the dove of peace, whose pure white breast has become colored purple-red with love, and whose head is crested with plumes of illumination. It is a royal bird, representing the expression and perfection of love and light. It is said to live to 500 or 600 years, or to over 1,000 years, at the end of which it fills its nest with spices in the top branches of a palm tree, the tree of life. Seated on this nest the phoenix turns it into a pyre by lighting it with the Sun's rays. The bird is consumed in the fire; but from the flames it rises up, reborn, rejuvenated. The phoenix life-span of over 1,000 years refers to half an astrological age, or one twenty-fourth of a Great Age. The 500–600 years is one half of this time period. That is to say, each successive life-span of the phoenix represents either one-half or one-quarter of an age: thus it is said that there are two or four phoenixes born in every age.

celestial north pole takes approximately 25,800 years to 26,000 years to complete its circle around the zodiacal center, and the zodiacal division of this circle means that each twelfth part, that relates to a sign of the zodiac, consists of approximately 2,160 years, the time period of each astrological age. And 270 years is one-eighth of 2,160 years, linking the cycles of the solar breath to the eight great festivals or power points of each age. (See figure 11, page 33.)

The Nine Breaths

Besides the solar wind cycle of twenty-six breaths there is a concurrent cycle of nine great breaths of the Sun that occur in a year, or in any cycle of time. These nine breaths are directly associated with inspiration from the spiritual aspect of the Sun. This is best illustrated by the Celtic story of the great goddess Ceridwen and her magic cauldron.

Ceridwen's bowl or cauldron is kept in a revolving four-cornered castle that has three names—the Castle of Revelry, the Crystal Castle, and the Castle of Riches. The castle sits on a high conical hill and has a circular moat (or lake) surrounding it. Nine maidens attend the cauldron, alternately applying their breath to keep the fire of inspiration burning beneath the cauldron. In this way, "for a year and a day," the keepers of the cauldron prepare a potion, a *greal* or grail.

The four-cornered castle on its hill, surrounded by the ring of water, signifies the Wheel of Life. The cauldron represents the cycle of the year consciously experienced; the grail is the knowledge gained as a result of that experience. The nine maidens symbolize nine spiritual impulses or

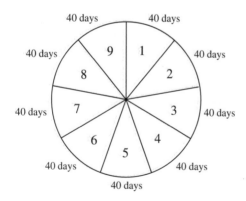

Figure 12. The Nine Great Breaths and Gates of Inspiration.

"breaths" that occur at forty-day intervals in each annual cycle. The moments of inspiration are known as the Nine Gates of Inspiration. In America these special moments in the year are celebrated by the Native Americans with their Ghost Dance, danced in a circle around a Peace Tree, planted at a significant place of power and representing the axis of the world. (See figure 12, page 34.)

THE LUNAR CYCLE

The idea of the thirteen months in a year is derived from the rhythmic cycle of the solar wind, but many people today and in the past have tried to attribute this to the lunar cycle of the Moon. The Moon is a kind of marker of the vital breathing of the Sun, but a very approximate and inaccurate one—the popular lunar cycle actually being based upon a lunation (i.e., the synodic period), which is the interval between successive New Moons. This interval is approximately twenty-nine-and-a-half days, a day-and-a-half longer than two complete solar breaths, which means that there are in fact only twelve complete lunar months in a year.

Nevertheless, the lunar cycle has its own strategic importance in our lives and the life of the planet, through the effect of the Moon's gravitational pull, and by modifying the effects of the solar wind and light. Among other things, the Moon has a polarizing effect on crystal structures, and largely governs the tides of the Earth's oceans and of water everywhere, including the water which composes a large part of our human bodies and those of animals and plants.

Unlike the Sun, the Moon is not a radiant life-giving form, but only a mirror-like rocky reflector of the Sun's light. Compared with the Sun, the Moon's influence is substantially different and subtle, and it is this subtlety which tends to have a sometimes powerful effect upon our psyche and sensitivity, for the psyche has a special ability to respond or react to small and subtle changes. In the worst extreme the Moon's influence can upset the minds and nervous systems of certain people to such an extent that they go mad, expressing what is commonly called lunacy. When this does happen, such irrational and unbalanced behavior seems to occur especially at Full Moons; yet to a great many other people the effect of Full Moons can be highly romantic or inspirational, and in a peak experience can be enlightening.

The subtle lunar cycles provide a kind of counterbalance and polarity to the powerful solar cycles, the former being described as watery and fluid, the latter as fiery and fixed, by comparison with each other. The one is life-receiving and reflective, the other life-giving and radiant. The former is associated with the fickle mind and psyche, the latter with the constant heart and soul, as portrayed so well in the hieroglyph of Mercury (see chapter 3, "Mercury").

The lunar cycles weave as it were a mysterious thread of silver light within the fiery gold framework of the solar cycles. Because they can have an influential effect upon the psyche, it can be helpful to recognize the lunar cycles and celebrate their festival times in an appropriate manner. Usually it is the Full Moon which is celebrated, when the effect of the Moon often increases our sensitivity and psychism, and the Moon, itself, is fully reflecting back to us the light of the Sun; although the New Moon can be equally powerful in another way. Like the annual solar cycle, a lunation is one complete cycle of time with its own seasons, known as the phases of the Moon. These four phases—New (or Dark) Moon, Waxing Moon, Full Moon and Waning Moon—correspond to the annual seasons of winter, spring, summer, and autumn. (See figure 13.)

When the months are counted from New Moon to New Moon, as was done by the Hebrews, and is still done by both the Jewish and Is-

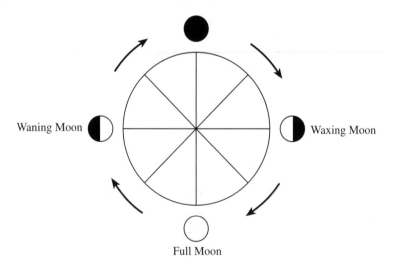

Figure 13. The Lunar Cycle.

lamic nations, the result gives twelve lunar months, totalling 354 days, in one year. Because there is a discrepancy of eleven days between the lunar year of 354 days and the solar year of 365 days, it means that the lunar calendar has to be readjusted every two to three years by adding in an extra lunar month. It takes nineteen solar years, or 235 lunar months, for the Moon to return to the same apparent position with regard to the Sun—a period known as the Metonic cycle, and used by the Druids as the basic period of Bardic training in their mystery schools.

The Full Moon phase is an excellent time for meditation and inner reflection, for intimate group work of a sensitive and psychic nature, for healing work, and for the reception and conception by the psyche of the wisdom of God, the light of Love. When the Full Moons correspond with the Solar Festivals, the effect is particularly powerful. In fact, as mentioned earlier, the Celts sometimes arranged for their Quarterday Solar Festivals to be marked by the Full Moons occurring nearest to the cusps of the seasons, so as to link the solar and lunar cycles and make use of the extra effect that this might have.

The Full Moons occur when the Moon appears in the sky on the opposite side of the Earth to the Sun; such that, for instance, when the Sun sets in the west the Full Moon rises in the east. Each Full Moon is related traditionally to the position of the Sun in the zodiac at the time of the Full Moon; so that, for example, the Aries Full Moon is the Full Moon that appears when the Sun is in the astrological sign of Aries, either at the time of or in the weeks following the Spring Equinox.

For thousands of years many of the great religions and cultures, East and West, have taken notice of the lunar cycle and celebrated the Full Moons with festivals whose meanings are related to the zodiac. Christianity, for instance, still celebrates Easter as a Full Moon festival, adopted from the Jewish Passover or Paschal Feast which marks the Aries Full Moon. Aries is the Paschal Ram or Lamb of God, representing the "first born" of God, the divine energy and light of love which is poured out for us in spring.

Balancing the Aries Full Moon, on the opposite side of the year, is Sukkoth, the Jewish "Season of Joy," marking the mid-autumn period and the Libra Full Moon, with its Yom Kippur, or "Day of Atonement," followed by the Feast of Tabernacles. The Day of Atonement, equivalent to the Christian Last Judgment, celebrated in Germany as the Buss-Bet-Tag, is when the Jewish nation confess their sins and ask for forgiveness—this occurring when the Sun is in Libra, the Balance, associated with the Last Judgment, when all hearts are weighed in the balance against the feather of truth. It is also the midpoint (or balance point) of the Jewish religious year, which begins with the month of Nisan, which contains the Aries Full Moon. The Libra Full Moon occurs in the seventh lunar month of Tishri; and, as the seventh month of the year, like the seventh day of the week, it is related to the Sabbath, the Day of Rest, when the Last Judgment is said to take place.

The Haj and Ramadan of Islam are likewise Full Moon festivals, as also are the great festivals of Hinduism and Buddhism—the Tripuri Purnima (Scorpio Full Moon) and Wessak (Taurus Full Moon). Polarizing the Full Moon festivals are the New Moon festivals. The series of Hindu festivals known as Shivaratri ("Night of Shiva"), for instance, celebrate each of the New Moons, with the three most powerful being the Maha-Shivaratri ("the Great Night of Shiva") at the Pisces New Moon, the Divali ("Festival of Lights") at the Libra New Moon, and the awesome Kali Puja ("Feast of Kali") at the Scorpio New Moon.

Nowadays, in our modern culture, there is a growing recognition of the importance of the three consecutive Full Moons which begin with the Aries Full Moon (Easter), followed by the Taurus Full Moon (Wessak) and the Gemini Full Moon (Christ Festival). These three Full Moons occur in the time period between the Spring Equinox and Midsummer, and constitute a trinity of Full Moon festivals relating to the life process of love, understanding, and service. Easter, for instance, reminds us of the perfect love, which cannot die, and which continually gives of itself that others might live; Wessak concerns the wisdom of that love, which brings understanding and illumination; and the Christ festival celebrates the loving, wise service that may be given to all humanity and all life.

In addition, this sequence relates to the initial descent of radiant spiritual energy from the crown of the head down toward the root of the spine and into the earth, to stir up the dragon of spiral earth energy: for Aries, Taurus, and Gemini are traditionally considered to be the zodiacal rulers of the head, throat, and shoulders respectively, with the remaining zodiacal signs governing the rest of the body in descending order, culminating with Pisces at the feet. (See further description in chapter 4.)

To celebrate the Full Moon festivals in a meditative way, with this progress in mind (*i.e.* of radiant energy descending stage by stage through the whole body like a baptism of light, from the top of the head down to the feet), is a wonderful and purifying experience, which can bring a deep inner joy and self-knowledge at the end of each twelve-month sequence.

THE HUMAN LIFE SPAN

It is possible to see a whole life span as one complete cycle, with a multitude of lesser cycles contained within it.

In the early years of each human life, once the basic physical form is established, the chief focus is on the development and training of our emotions and desires. In the next stage of life, the focus is on training the mind, and developing an understanding of life generally, and of our life purpose in particular. In the following, more mature stage, we enter into the major activity of our life and acquire the power to put our ideas and plans into practice.

Finally, there is old age, in which we have the chance to look back over our life experience, and either to be thankful and joyful for a life well spent, or to ask forgiveness (of God, others and ourselves) for that which was not well done. In either case we gain knowledge, real knowledge, and the transforming grace of universal love is always bestowed on those who are truly contrite. The very acts of asking for, receiving and granting forgiveness evoke love, and enable new cycles to emerge, based on love.

There are several subsidiary cycles within each complete life cycle, one of the most powerful being the 56-year cycle. This particular cycle is associated with Saturn, whose apparent revolution about the Earth (*i.e.* moving in a complete circle through the twelve signs of the zodiac) takes approximately 28–29 years, and which symbolically is associated with the number 7 and the seventh day of the week, the Sabbath. In this 56-year cycle there are seven years between each of the main festivals. Thus, when we are born at the "Christmas" of the cycle, our 7th birthday marks the Festival of Dedication, our 14th is at the Festival of Promise in the midspring of our youth, and our 21st "Coming of Age" occurs at the Mayday Festival of Unification.

Not only are these four moments in our lives usually very memorable (birth, ego-foundation, puberty, maturity), but so also are the other power points of this cycle. At 28 we are often at the height of our intellectual powers (but not necessarily wise); and 35 usually marks a major transformation in our lives. Around the age of 35 we often seem to come into our real life's work, or our work becomes properly established. The ages of 42 and 49 are the well-known "death" periods of the ego: 42 corresponding to the main harvest festival of the cycle, which can precipitate the so-called "dark night of the soul." But ultimately this is a good thing, for once we are through the darkness and terror that such a power point in time can induce, the true fruit of our being, with its seed of light, will remain, much strengthened, while most of the psychological dross that is not needed any more will have been removed, consumed by nature's "fire."

Age 49 brings one to the point of Samhain, the Festival of Peace. Here takes place a second death of the ego, but it usually manifests as a fundamental change of life—a letting go of an old form of life or way of being, maybe a change of job or a change in personal circumstances. At this time (49–50) men especially reach a crisis point concerning their work, and women often undergo an equivalent crisis concerning their physiological and family purpose. It is possible for each of us to feel old and tired at this stage, and to "give up." This kind of decision will mean a slow and gradual degeneration of all faculties and interest in life, into old age and physiological death. But if we should awaken to the idea that life can start again at 50, then it will. After due preparation and acclimatization, including the remembrance of and thanksgiving for what life has given us so far, at 56 the second 56–year cycle will provide a new "Christmas," and fresh energies and inspiration can flow in. (See fig. 14.)

If taken in the right spirit—which, of course, is helped when we have good health and some understanding of what is going on—these crisis

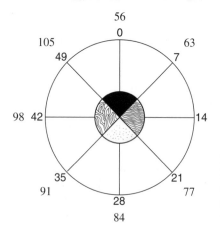

Figure 14. The 56-Year "Saturn" Cycle.

Saturn is the Great Initiator. Every seven years in our lives corresponds to a Solar Festival and gate of initiation in the Saturnian life cycle.

points can be taken in our stride and be made to work for us, not against us; for then we will be "dancing" with the Wheel of Life.

Step-by-step, cycle-by-cycle, each one of us may gradually master the Wheel of Life. The final state of illumination is experienced as joy or bliss, which transforms and illuminates not just the mind, but also the body—hence the vitality, the shining eyes and skin, and the halo of the saints.

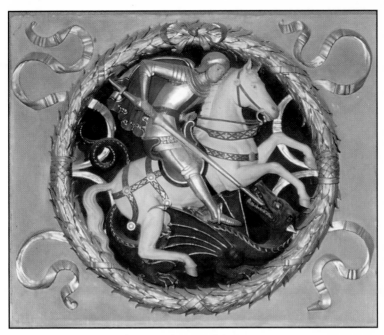

Plate 1. St. George and the Dragon.
Painted sculpture on wall of Southwark Cathedral, London, England.
Photograph by Suzy Straw.

Plate 3 (above). The Archangel Michael.
Altarpiece. Kranj, Slovenia. Photograph by author.

Plate 2 (left). Crucifixion.
Painting by Raphael,
The National Gallery, London. Ref. 3943.

Plate 5 (above). The Heart of Lothian.
The Royal Mile, Edinburgh, Scotland. Photograph by John Dawkins.

Plate 4 (left). Madonna and Christ Child.
Sculpture of the Madonna and Child, Mallonca, France.
Photograph by Sue Taylor.

Plate 6. The Royal Mile, Edinburgh.
View looking up toward St. Giles' Cathedral. Photograph by John Dawkins.

Plate 7. Edinburgh Castle.
View from Princes Street Gardens. Photograph by John Dawkins.

Plate 8. Town Center, Stein-am-Rhein.
Photograph by Marianne Rieke.

Plate 9. Heart of Berlin.
The Marx-Engels Forum, Palace of the Republic and Berlin Cathedral, with
the Unter den Linden Avenue shooting like an arrow into the distance.
Photograph by author.

Plate 10. The Mall, Washington, DC.
View of the Washington Memorial looking west down the Mall
from the Capitol.
Photograph by author.

Plate 11. Lincoln Memorial, Washington, DC.
View of the Lincoln Memorial from the southeast.
Photograph by author.

Plate 12. The Long Reflecting Pool, Washington, DC.
View from the Lincoln Memorial looking east toward the
Washington Monument and Capitol in the distance.
Photograph by author.

Plate 13. The Capitol, Washington, DC.
View from Maryland Avenue, looking northeast.
Photograph by author.

Plate 14. The White House, Washington, DC.
North facade and fountain. Photograph by author.

Plate 15. The Dragon Rocks. The Externsteine, Germany.
Photograph by Dominic McManus.

Plate 16. The Crucified Man. The Externsteine, Germany.
Photograph by Marianne Rieke.

Plate 17. Niagara Falls, New York.
View looking south toward New York State from the Canadian side.
Photograph by author.

Plate 18. Squaw Island, Canandaigua Lake.
Canandaigua Finger Lake, New York State. View looking south across the lake
from the north shore toward the much-eroded Squaw Island.
Photograph by author.

Plate 19. Onondaga Lake.
The Finger Lakes, New York State. View looking southward toward Big Hill
and Syracuse from the site of Hiawatha's village. Photograph by author.

Plate 20. Sunset behind Mt. Tamalpais.
View across San Francisco Bay from Indian Rock.
Photograph by author.

Plate 21. The Golden Gate.
View of Golden Gate Bridge looking south toward San Francisco.
Photograph by author.

Plate 22. Europa and the Bull.
Fountain sculpture at Halmstad, Germany.

Plate 23. "The Heart of the Bow."
Rainbow Lake, Cottonwood Pass, Southern Rockies, Colorado.
Photograph by author.

THREE

Space and the Form of Life

Nothing retains its own form; but Nature, the great renewer, ever makes up forms from forms. Be sure there's nothing perishes in the whole Universe; it does but vary and renew its form.

—Ovid

THE CIRCLE OF SPACE

The process of life, with its cycle of time, takes place within a form of life. All life forms exist within, and are formed out of space. Just as time has its cycles, so space has its circles or horizons. We each have our own space and need our own space, with its horizon or boundary of consciousness and sensitivity. All forms of life are similar in this respect, even man-made ones. Often this space is so important to us that we are prepared to fight over it, to prevent others invading what we consider to be our space; not realizing that not only is it possible to share space, but that we do this all the time with a host of other beings, seen and unseen. The ultimate description of space and of the life form inhabiting that space, which is Universal Being, is of the center which is everywhere within a circle that is nowhere. (See figure 15, page 60.)

There is an intimate relationship between the cycle of time and the circle of space, and most people have no trouble in seeing this clearly. For example, in the northern hemisphere we normally associate winter with night, and with cold and darkness, qualities associated with the north. We link spring with the morning, with the rising Sun, and

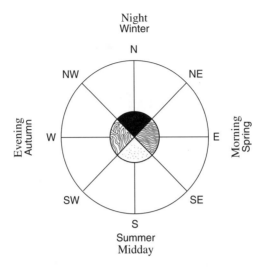

Figure 15. The Circle of Space (Seasons + Elements + NSEW + Quarter-directions).
The eight major festivals relate to the eight major points of the compass.

therefore with the east where the Sun rises. Summer we associate with midday, and with the greatest warmth and brightness, and therefore with the south where the Sun shines most brightly and is at its greatest height in the sky. Autumn, the final season of the year, is associated with evening and the setting Sun, and therefore with the west where the Sun sets. Midwinter is thus related to due north, Midsummer to due south, the Spring Equinox to due east, and the Autumn Equinox to due west. The Quarterdays are, respectively, related to the northeast, southeast, southwest and northwest.

These relationships are important, for they have a bearing on how we are affected sublimally by the effect of orientation within our horizon, or circle of space. For instance, the north is, by analogy, linked with the element *earth*, with birth and gestation, and with the human life impulse that begins each cycle of life. For this reason the north gate is considered to be the gate by which we enter incarnation, and by which we leave it at the end of our lifespan. The North Pole Star, symbolized by the six-pointed Blazing Star or Christ Star, is known as the Alpha and Omega, our guiding light and the place from which we come, and to which we return again after death. Traditionally the priest, before taking mass or holy communion, is supposed to come from the north side of the altar; and the pilgrim's door in any temple or church is the north door. The pilgrim (in Freemasonry, the freemason) treads his initial circuitous path "clockwise" or "sunwise" from the north to the east, to the south, and then to the west, imitating the Sun as it moves in its (apparent) circuit in the sky.

Likewise, the east is linked with the element *water*, with emotion and the energy of love, the creative life force, known also as the Word or Wisdom of God. Christian churches, and many temples of other religions and cultures, are purposely oriented with their "heads" (chancels) pointing toward the east, so that the energies of love-wisdom may enter the church through the crown of the church and descend the axis of the church from crown to root, east to west, thus identifying the spiritual energy of the church with the life energies of the east. (The kundalini or dragon energies which rise up the axis of the church are then associated with the west.)

The south is linked with the element *air*, and with thought and illumination of the mind; and the west with the element *fire*, with outer activity or manifestation (in the form of service or charity), the fruit of the cycle. As for the quarter-directions, they are associated with the Quarterdays, the Cherubim and the four gates to Paradise.

The influences from all these directions of space are constantly affecting us. It matters, for instance, which way we lie when we sleep, and it is important for each of us to find which orientation is most comfortable for our own individual needs. Different orientations emphasize different levels or types of consciousness.

THE ZODIAC

Besides the four main quarters and the eight major directions of space, there is also the zodiac or twelvefold division of space. *Zodiac* means "circle of creatures," and is the name given to an imaginary band extending 9° each side of the ecliptic, or Sun's path in the sky, and along which are to be found twelve constellations. These twelve zodiacal constellations divide the sky into twelve divisions—divisions which are unequal in astronomical terms, but made to be equal in astrological symbolism. The Sun and most of the planets pass through these constellations in turn. The Sun travels through all twelve constellations and thus round the whole circle of the ecliptic in one year; the planets take

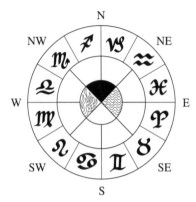

Figure 16. The Zodiac Temple.

longer, each having its own time period in which it completes the cycle. The constellations are associated with mythological beings or creatures that are used as symbols to describe allegorically the effect that time and space have upon us, and the intelligence and type of energy that lie behind the phenomenon. (See figure 16, above.)

The archetypal (*i.e.* astrological) pattern of time, when related to the circle of space, links the four principal directions to the cusps of signs that mark the solstices and equinoxes of the year: hence due north lies on the cusp of Sagittarius-Capricornus, east lies on the cusp of Pisces-Aries, south on the cusp of Gemini-Cancer, and west on the cusp of Virgo-Libra. The quarter directions, therefore, coincide with the midpoints of the "fixed" signs of the Zodiac—Aquarius in the northeast, Taurus in the southeast, Leo in the southwest and Scorpio in the northwest. From this is derived the archetypal symbols of the four cherubic gatekeepers of Paradise—the man-faced Cherub (Aquarius) at the first gate, the bull-faced Cherub (Taurus) at the second gate, the lion-faced Cherub (Leo) at the third gate, and the eagle-faced Cherub (Scorpio) at the final gate.

The zodiacal attributes of the circle of space help us to understand in an even more detailed way the meaning and effect of the different directions of space.

GEOMETRIC PATTERNS

All the various rhythms of time are expressed in the circle of space, each with their own meaning and unique power and effect upon us. Each has a geometric expression, for geometry lies at the heart of all form.

The circle of space is commonly divided into 360° (degrees), each quarter having 90° and each zodiacal division being 30°. This division does not relate easily to the annual cycle of time, which has approximately 365 days in a year, but it is a practical geometric division which does, at the same time, embody the unique signature of humanity. The five extra days are absorbed into the 360° by spreading them evenly throughout the circle, with the "Day out of Time" coinciding with the north direction. The positions where they occur not only divide the circle into five equal portions, but form the points of a pentagram or five-pointed star, the special signature of this planet and humanity. The five-petalled rose is associated symbolically with the pentagram, as the emblem of love expressed through the human being.

This fivefold pattern is also associated with the planet Venus, which makes in an eight-year period an apparent "dance" around the Earth that sketches out the pattern of an intricate five-petalled rose. Mythologically, therefore, the Earth, Venus and the rose are linked together, and we use both the rose and Venus to symbolize human love. (See figure 17.)

The twelve-month rhythm represented by the twelve zodiacal signs has a geometry based upon the equilateral triangle. The triangle drawn twice, each one interpenetrating the other and lying in opposite directions, gives the hexagram or six-pointed Blazing Star. When repeated

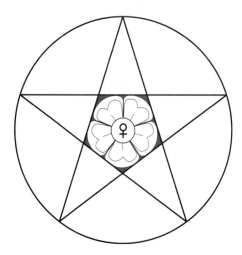

Figure 17. The Pentagram and Rose of Venus.

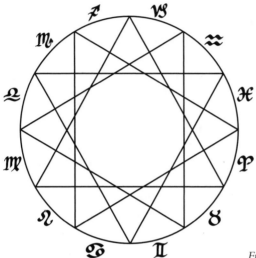

Figure 18. The Zodiac Star.

again, with its axis turned through 90°, the resulting figure gives the twelve-pointed star. (See figure 18.)

The triangle is a symbol of the Trinity and is related to the planet Mercury, which traces approximately three loops in a "shamrock" design in its apparent annual orbit about the Earth. For this reason Mercury is associated symbolically with the Holy Trinity, and thus with the Sun

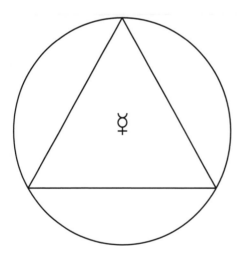

Figure 19. The Triangle and Dance of Mercury.

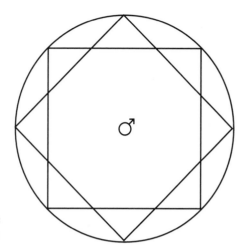

*Figure 20. The Octagram
and Dance of Mars.*

and the sun-god or hero, who is crucified in space (*i.e.* spread out in the four principal directions) to become the twelve creatures or signs of the zodiac, each of which he experiences in turn. (See figure 19, page 64.)

In a pattern of more exactness, Mercury returns to the same position in the sky in its apparent circuit around the Earth after tracing twenty-two loops—a significant number associated with the number of paths on the Cabalistic Tree of Life diagram and represented by the twenty-two Major Arcana cards of the tarot. Jupiter has a kind of relationship with this, performing eleven loops in the course of its twelve-year dance about the Earth.

The eightfold division of the circle, associated with the eight major directions of space and the corresponding eight Solar Festivals, is described geometrically by the octagon and the eight-pointed star (octagram). This geometry is linked with the planet Mars, the planet associated symbolically with the Law of God, which describes eight loops about the Earth in a fifteen-year geocentric orbit. (See figure 20.)

The temporal rhythms that are manifested in the orbital patterns of Mercury, Venus and Mars form a beautiful sequence of relationships (3:5:8) which is known philosophically as the Golden Proportion or Golden Mean, and designated by the 21st letter of the Greek alphabet (ϕ). Mathematically it is known as the Fibonacci Series, which begins 1:1:2:3:5:8:13:21, etc. For thousands of years this proportion has dominated art and architecture, and is expressed powerfully in the growth patterns of nature. Wherever there is a particular harmony and beauty

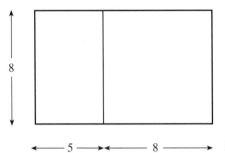

8

←— 5 —→←——— 8 ———→   *Figure 21. The Golden Proportion.*

of form this proportion will be found. Three good examples can be readily seen in the form of the beautiful conch shell and the distribution of seeds in the sunflower, each of which manifests a Golden Mean logarithmic spiral, and the measure of a human being, whose total height is divided by the navel in the Golden Proportion. (See figure 21.)

The planet Saturn, which describes twenty-eight loops in its 29-year apparent journey about the Earth, is the Greek Cronos, or Pan—"Old Father Time," who is said to rule the time cycle and who plays the seven-fluted pan-pipes. These pipes are related both to the 7-day weekly cycle of Solar Breath, the octave in music, and to the twenty-eight loops of Saturn's journey around the Earth which forms the points of a heptagram or seven-pointed star repeated four times in the four main directions. (See figures 22 and 23.)

Figure 22. The Heptagram.

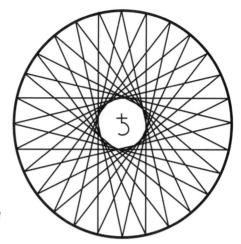

*Figure 23. The 28-Pointed
Star: The Dance of Pan.*

Significant patterns are also made by the conjunctions and oppositions of the planets, the most notable being that of Jupiter and Saturn.
The cycle of conjunctions between the two planets is approximately
twenty years. Three successive conjunctions mark out the corners of an
equilateral triangle in a 60-year period. The oppositions of Saturn and
Jupiter also occur every twenty years, and in a 60-year period they mark
out the six points of a six-pointed star—the Christ Star or Star of David,
also known in Freemasonry as the Blazing Star.

Conjunctions of Saturn and Jupiter which occur in the constellation
of Pisces are said in Jewish (and Babylonian) tradition to herald important occurrences; and, if conjunct with Mars also, it heralds or marks a
significant birth or appearance on Earth of the spirit of the Messiah, as
the "Fish Savior." Triple conjunctions (in any zodiacal constellation) are
even more rare, occurring approximately every 139 years (i.e., 7 x 20
years). Very significantly, the birth of Christ Jesus of Nazareth was
marked or heralded, in 7 B.C., by a rare triple Saturn-Jupiter conjunction
in the sign of Pisces during which Mars was also conjunct.

THE HUMAN BODY

One of the most beautiful forms of life is the human body, the material
vehicle through which the soul expresses itself. Like all the forms of nature, its basic substance is matter, which is the natural polarity to spirit,

but matter released as earth energy and built into a suitable form, a work of architecture. In Zoence we understand the body as being not only physical, but also composed of finer, more subtle energy bodies associated with the human psyche.

The form of the body relates directly to the life process, just as in all good architecture the architectural form expresses the function and enables the function to take place in the best possible way. For example, in our body the most important components—the head, chest, and abdomen—can be recognized as a trinity. We can survive without arms or legs (although of course they are extremely useful!), but we could not survive without any one of these vital three. They form three linked but distinct parts, united by the spine and functioning as one. Their very structure expresses the law of trinity and the threefold process of life.

For instance, the head is composed of a hard skull which has little flexibility but is highly protective, and which is set above the chest. Below the chest, the abdomen is soft and flexible, making a polarity to the head. In the middle, sharing the qualities of both head and abdomen, is the chest with its ribcage, which is partly flexible and partly rigid. This contains the true midpoint between the two poles of abdomen and head.

From this midpoint, deep within the center of our being, arise the inner impulses that lead to the various cycles of desire-thought-action taking place within our body. The impulse, originally buried in our hearts, invisible and secret, is first expressed as emotion, or, ideally, as love. In the body, love is clearly related to the heart and to the chest which protects it. In fact, all the principal organs of love and life (the breath of love) are contained in the chest, as the heart and lungs.

Thinking is, of course, associated with the head, which contains all the principal organs of thought or perception. The third part of the life process, action, is related to the abdomen. This area is like an engine-house; it is our generative center, the seat of our willpower and of our procreative ability, not only to produce physical bodies for our children, but, more generally, to put ideas into practice.

Thus our bodies themselves are designed architecturally to contain and express the three stages of desire, thought, and action, which are all equally important, and which, through conscious work on ourselves, can be transformed into love, understanding, and service. This in turn has the power to keep the body healthy, and ultimately to transmute its very nature into light. (See figure 24, page 69.)

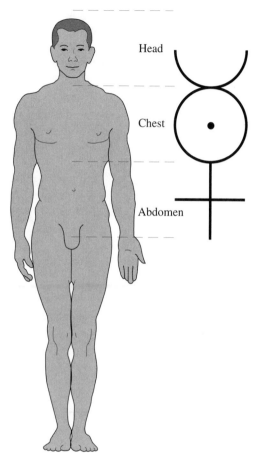

Figure 24. The Body as a Trinity/Mercury.

MERCURY

One beautiful and succinct way of understanding and remembering the architectural secret of the body was devised by the ancient sages: namely, the hieroglyph of Mercury. The hieroglyph of Mercury (the name originates from the Ancient Egyptian *Maa Kheru*, meaning "The True Word") is composed of three distinct symbols representing the Sun, the Moon, and the cross of the elements. The Sun symbol (the circle with a dot in the center), signifying the life-giving principle of radiant light, lies in the middle. Placed above it is the crescent Moon, representing the principle of reflection; while lying below the Sun is the Cross, emblem not only of the four alchemical elements of matter, but of self-sacrifice.

The Sun with its life-giving light is equated with love, which is the creative and illuminating life-force. The dot in the center of the Sun denotes the source of that light—the impulse from which all else arises. The Moon, reflecting the light of the Sun, personifies the mind or intellect, which is like a mirror reflecting the light of the heart, for all thinking is a perception or "seeing," all seeing is a reflection, and all thought-forms or ideas are images. The Cross represents the world of matter in which the idea must be put into action as service, which is a self-sacrifice made in love.

This hieroglyph of Mercury is an architectural plan of all temples— human, natural and man-made—and represents the cosmos itself.

THE MOVEMENT OF THE LIFE PROCESS

The movement of the life process through the body is from the heart to the head to the abdomen and back to the heart. This gives an additional energy flow to the two already mentioned: namely the spiritual energy which descends the spine from the crown of the head and the earth (or dragon) energy which ascends through the body from the base of the spine. A figure-of-eight (8) is used to denote this third energy flow, which is like the child of its parents, and which, for this reason, is referred to in Zoence as the soul energy or mercurial energy.

The figure-of-eight blood flow in the physical body imitates the flow of soul energy; and, for similar reasons, the blood is traditionally associated with the soul. The **8** is a sign or signature of Mercury, and also of what is known as the Holy Spirit or Breath. Sometimes referred to as the cosmic lemniscate, nowadays we use it as a sign of infinity; but its meaning is associated with eternal life—continual regeneration and transmutation through purification and inspiration, roles which the blood imitates in the human body. It is also the figure used for the number 8, the number of the spokes of the Wheel of Life. For these reasons, in churches both the font (signifying baptism or purification) and the pulpit (signifying inspiration and the Word of God) are octagonal.

THE CHAKRAS

Lying along the human spine are seven major chakras, or energy centers. These naturally appear as soon as the trinity is expressed in form, as in the human form. For instance, each of the three main areas of the body (head, chest, abdomen) has a center. The two places where the main areas connect form two more chakras; and then there is a top and bottom—the two poles of the life form. These add up to seven. Geometrically we can arrive at the same result by drawing three circles that touch

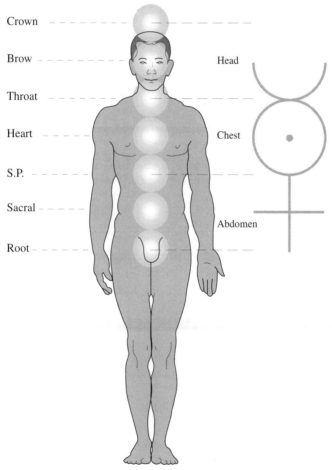

Figure 25. The Chakras.

each other on a straight line. The three centers on the line, plus the four places where the circles touch each other and cross the line give the seven focal points. (See figure 25, page 71.)

The chakras at the centers of the head, chest, and abdomen are known today as the brow, heart, and sacral chakras, respectively. The chakra situated between the head and the chest is called the throat chakra, and the chakra between the chest and the abdomen is named the solar plexus chakra. The crown and root chakras are the names of the two poles, at the top of the head and the base of the spine.

In India, teachings about these seven chakras of the spine have usually been quite readily available, but in the West, although there has always been knowledge of these energy foci, this knowledge has been kept a guarded secret, veiled in allegory and symbolism. These seven major chakras, which are powerful focal points in the energy bodies of human beings and nature, are linked with and govern the workings of the major plexi, glands, and organs of the body. They are also associated with seven different types and levels of consciousness. There are, in addition, numerous minor chakras. Nowadays many books and teachings exist about the chakras, usually from the Eastern perspective and many of them quite complex; but simply considering the geometry of the human body in conjunction with the life process working within it will help you to understand the function of each chakra.

In addition to the seven major chakras there is an "eighth," the alta major chakra, located at the nape of the neck. Also called the Pan chakra, it is associated with universal consciousness, hence its name. It acts as a control chakra, and integrates the powers and qualities of all the other chakras. It is the primary gateway for divine inspiration to enter the heart, breathed in, as it were, via the gateway of the alta major from the heart of our higher self. The physical breath is an echo of this spiritual breath. The alta major chakra is a center that we should care for: it is perhaps the most sensitive area of the whole body. Wearing a silk scarf, or a high collar, or even just placing a hand over the back of the neck when necessary, can be a good protection. Washing the back of the neck under a cool shower of water does wonders.

THE HUMAN ZODIAC

Besides the chakras, the energy body of the human being has within it a zodiac which governs and manifests as twelve distinct areas of the physical body. The zodiacal arrangement is such that Aries rules the

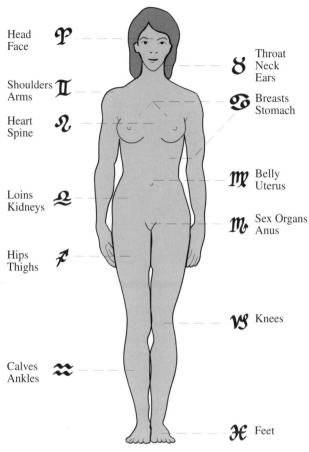

Head
Face ♈

Throat
Neck ♉
Ears

Shoulders ♊
Arms

Breasts ♋
Stomach

Heart ♌
Spine

Belly ♍
Uterus

Loins ♎
Kidneys

Sex Organs ♏
Anus

Hips ♐
Thighs

Knees ♑

Calves ♒
Ankles

Feet ♓

Figure 26. The Zodiac in the Human Body.

head and Pisces the feet, with the rest of the Zodiac laid out in order in between. Figure 26 shows the zodiacal correspondences.

It can be seen from this that the beginning and end of the sequence lies between Pisces and Aries, the cusp which is associated with the east direction and the Spring Equinox.

A whole science exists concerning the relationship of a person's physiology and health to these zodiacal areas of the human body. (See figure 27, page 74.)

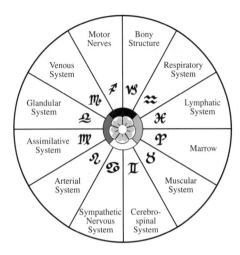

Figure 27. Zodiacal Physiology.

One very powerful pattern of health is that which is connected to the "fixed" zodiacal signs associated with the four Cherubim, the Gate-keepers of Paradise. This truth is enshrined in myth and allegory, one of the key allegories being that of the Grail King. Like a Shakespearean play, all the characters of the story can be understood as being aspects of our own self.

It is said that, through the misdemeanours of mankind, the Grail King suffers three great wounds—one to the throat, one to the heart, and one to the groin. (See figure 28.) While he lies wounded the Grail Kingdom lies waste, and the Holy Grail cannot be enjoyed. The Grail King waits for the hero, the Grail Knight, to recognize and heal the wounds and thereby bring the Grail Kingdom to life and prosperity once again.

Each wound is associated with a particular wrong or lack of some kind, and can only be healed by righting that wrong and manifesting what is lacking. The wounds also have to be healed in the same order in which they manifest.

The first wound is to the throat, and is the result of a lack of love. Taurus is the ruler of the throat and the muscular system, and is the Cherub that guards the second gate to Paradise, the Cherub who challenges us to see if we are truly loving before we are allowed to pass that gate. Learning to love is the first degree of initiation, the foundation

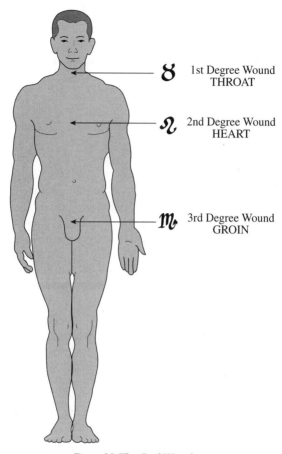

1st Degree Wound
THROAT

2nd Degree Wound
HEART

3rd Degree Wound
GROIN

Figure 28. The Grail Wounds.

upon which all the rest is built. A lack of love brings fear, and fear causes the neck and shoulder muscles to tighten, the throat to constrict and go dry, the tongue to either seize up or go out of control, and, in the worst case of panic, for us to seemingly "lose our heads." Love casts out fear: it develops in us an unshakeable courage and an intuitive rapport with all people, all things. A lack of love leads us to think and act out of fear, with a self-centered desire for self-preservation at all costs; and this itself can magnify to become greed, aggression, and even cruelty.

The second wound is to the heart and is the result of a lack of understanding. Even if we are loving people, we still need to develop an understanding of each other and life, or else grave mistakes can be made. The heart and arterial system are ruled by Leo, the Cherub of the third gate to Paradise, who challenges us as to whether we truly understand before allowing us past the gate. Learning to understand is the second degree of initiation. A lack of understanding affects the heart: a cold, over-critical mind can freeze the heart, anger can burn it, and jealousy can tear a heart to pieces.

The third wound is to the groin, and this is caused by a lack of service. The groin, containing the sexual organs and sacral chakra, is associated with our willpower and ability to get things done—not only to make love and procreate, but to put our desires and ideas into action. Scorpio, the Cherub of the fourth gate, governs the sex organs, the venous system, and all sexual matters. The secret of Scorpio, and of sex, is intimately connected with the dragon energy, and with raising it right up the spine to the crown of the head, bringing ecstatic joy and enlightenment. This only occurs when the person is acting in service, out of love and with understanding, in a powerful, devoted and focused way. If the actions are selfish, uncharitable, and hurtful to others, the sexual dragon energy will become trapped and distorted, and the groin will become wounded. Taken to the extreme, it can lead to such perverse actions as violent rape, which is really about exerting power by force over others, severely wounding others, as well as being badly wounded oneself.

The secret of Scorpio and of the last gateway is concerned with the depths and the heights of experience. The scorpion signifies the depths, and the eagle (the higher symbolism of Scorpio) represents the heights. The serpent, another symbol of Scorpio, represents the awakened and rising dragon energy, which then transmutes into the winged eagle, soaring into the light of the Sun and seeing all things. The fourth symbol of Scorpio is the dove, the final state of transmutation, the emblem of peace and illumination. Scorpio is the sign of death and resurrection, the final stage of transmutation leading to true peace, which is Paradise. Passing this gate can only be done by the person who truly serves; hence the motto of the Grail knight is, "I serve."

RIGHT-HAND AND LEFT-HAND

Besides the vertical polarity in our human form, there is the horizontal left-right polarity which is important to consider. Except for left-handed people who are the exception to the rule, the right hand is associated with giving and with creativity, and the left hand with receiving and with sensitivity. This appears to be an archetypal pattern, and was symbolized by the sages with the emblems of Sun and Moon, utilizing the same Mercurial symbols to show this polarity of right and left, and their relationships to the rest of the human being.

The Sun is associated with the right hand and the whole right-hand side of the body, as the Sun is a giver of energy, a radiator of light. The left hand and the left-hand side of the body is represented by the Moon, a receiver of energy and reflector of light. (See Plate 2, page 44.)

The receptivity of a person is associated with feeling and sensitivity, and with the mind or intellect, which responds to emotion and reflects the light of the heart: hence the left-hand side is linked with the mind and the head, of which the Moon is the symbol. The creativity of a person is associated with the forceful giving out of energy, as emotion or love, and with the heart or soul, which radiates love and speaks the truth creatively; and so the right-hand side is linked with the soul, and with the heart and throat, of which the Sun is the symbol. (See figure 29, below.)

The same symbolism also applies in explaining the polarity within the heart, to which the throat is linked, and the polarity within the head. The polarity of the heart is wisdom and intelligence—the inner teacher and the intuition—represented by Sun and Moon respectively. The polarity of the head is imagination and reason, or conceptualization

Figure 29. Heart of Love and Eye of Perception.
Emblem XXV from Daniel Cramer's book of emblems, *Societas Iesu et Roseae Crucis Vera—Emblematum Sacrorum,* 1617.

and organization (including analysis), represented likewise as Sun and Moon respectively. But the whole of the heart or soul is a sun in contrast to the whole of the head or mind which is a moon to the heart-sun.

Other symbols have been used to help explain this polarity, such as a heart associated with the right hand, and an eye (representing the mind and head) associated with the left hand. In Hebraic-Christian symbolism, Moses the prophet is associated with the right-hand side, and Aaron the high priest with the left-hand side. The one speaks and reveals the Word of Wisdom, the other receives the teaching and organizes it into a form that can be put to practical use. The one brings inspiration and vision, the other checks it academically and manages it. (See figure 30, page 79.)

This is also represented by the symbolism of the Christ giving a blessing with his raised right hand while holding a book, the receptacle of wisdom, in his left. We use our right hands in a similar way, to give blessings to each other when waving or shaking hands, for instance, or giving a healing touch. (See figure 31, page 80.)

In the symbolism of St. Michael, or St. George, the angel-knight holds a spear (or sword) in his right hand and a shield in his left. The spear signifies the ray of light, while the shield, which is polished as a mirror, represents the reflective mind. Similar to this is the symbolism of the king or queen, who holds a scepter of power in the right hand and an orb of dominion in the left. (See Plate 3, page 45.)

The cross, signifying action, is what unites the other two. Heart and mind, Sun and Moon, are united and "married" when love and understanding are put into practice as service.

Another way of understanding strife and friendship is as the mind and heart: the mind strives to understand, the heart loves as a friend. When balanced and united together they create harmony. Harmony then produces beauty, and beauty evokes the final manifestation of love as joy. The cross of service is what brings this about.

Human society tends to divide itself in a fashion which echoes this pattern, for some people are more heart-oriented and some more intellectually inclined. Some prefer action. The heart-oriented people are usually the more poetic and intuitive people, people who feel called to serve as healers, doctors, nurses, teachers, and artists, for instance. The head-oriented people are usually the ones good at organizing and administrating, at facts and figures, numbers and accounts. They usually

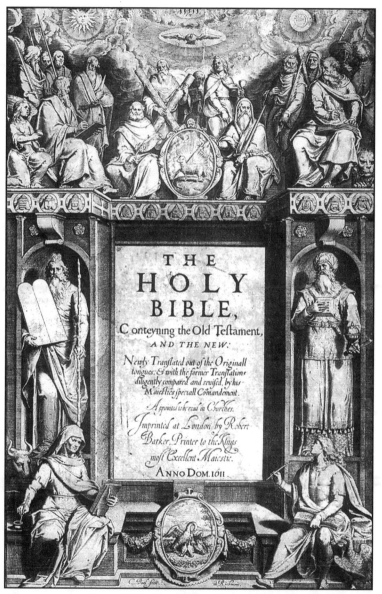

Figure 30. The Two Pillars—Moses and Aaron.
Title page of the 1611 King James I Authorized Version of the Holy Bible. The
British Library. Ref. c.35.L.13(1).

Figure 31. Christ in Glory.
Carving above the West Door of the Royal Portal, Chartres Cathedral, France.
Photograph by author.

make up the bulk of politicians, industrialists, bankers, lawyers, accountants, managers, and so on.

At the moment there is a definite tilt toward the left-hand of society, with more importance given to the intellectual, organizational, managerial skills than to the healing and teaching professions, while the real value of art and poetry, and of intuition, is virtually ignored. If we want harmony and beauty in society and our lives, and the resulting joy, then we need to find the balance in ourselves and in our society.

THE CELESTIAL BODY

As love manifests from the heart as the creative life-force, it immediately sets up the polarities of being, the crown chakra with its spiritual energy and the root chakra with its earth energy. These two energies constantly interact during the whole process of life, like father and mother, to create the child, the soul.

When a person experiences a spiritual awakening, radiant energy descends like a rod of lightning from crown to root, stirring up the earth energy which sleeps at the base of the spine like a coiled serpent. Once it is stirred awake, it begins to spiral up the spine, eventually bursting through the crown at the top of the head. How much this energy rises, and to what extent it bursts through the crown of the head, depends upon how well we are performing the life process. To those with clairvoyant vision it looks like a fountain of clear water, shooting upward and then arching over above the head to fall in glittering light back to the ground. Its shape is the origin of the wings that we accord to angels. The glittering effect, which looks like millions of twinkling stars, inspired the name given to this highly spiritualized form of the soul—the celestial body. (See figure 32.)

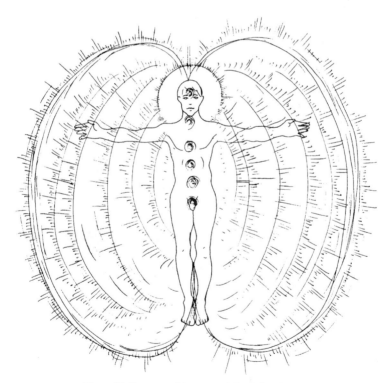

Figure 32. Fountain of Energy and the Celestial Body.

Where the fountain of energy bursts through the dome of the head it appears like three plumes of white light, to which is given the name of "dove" (as it looks rather like a pure white dove hovering over and descending upon the head). This, together with the halo, is our spiritual crown, achieved when we have found the joy of illumined peace. The trident symbolizes this phenomenon of the fountain of earth energy with the "dove" at the top. In the East it is known as Shiva's trishul. The crown of the Prince of Wales, with its three feathers, is a more modern representation, derived, some say, from the fleur-de-lis which once symbolized this shining crown of the enlightened human soul.

Because, when this happens, the chakras are each shining with light like miniature suns and a halo has appeared around the head, rays of light are shooting through the winged aura, creating rainbows of color and appearing like "feathers" of light. The colorful feathered headdresses of many native peoples are physical representations of this more subtle and evolved energy form, the form of the enlightened soul. The effect of the rainbow light creates what is known as the aureole (or flame shape) around the body—a spiritual aura which is often depicted in Christian art by pictures of the Christ in glory, or of the Mother Mary blessing the world, and in Buddhist art by the almond-shaped aura around the Buddha.

A similar fountain of energy rises from the ground when the chakra points of the Earth are tended in love, and the spiritual energy of the cosmos awakens the serpent energy of the Earth. Pilgrimage with sacred, joyful song and dance are ways of stimulating and evolving these wonderful living structures of light, that are in effect part of the spiritualization of the very body of the Earth.

Man-made Forms

Man is the living temple of God,
and the heart is the Holy of Holies of that temple.
—MANLY P. HALL

The great architects of past civilizations understood the cosmic patterns and the effects of energy on consciousness and behavior. They knew how such knowledge could be used to create harmony in both buildings and the environment. In ancient times, architecture was a sacred and profound science which harmonized and embraced all other sciences and arts, acknowledging everything that existed as alive and intelligent. Complete cities and even whole countries were often laid out with a recognition of correct siting and chakras within the landscape.

This ancient wisdom has been lost or ignored in latter years, but there are signs that it is now being rediscovered and once again put into practice. One of the purposes of Zoence is to encourage this revival by making the ancient knowledge better known and understood, coupled with modern knowledge.

SACRED ARCHITECTURE

The sacred buildings and temples of different world traditions used to be consciously designed to incorporate the same beautiful patterns of energy that are found not only in the human body but also in the rest of nature. The pre-Reformation Christian churches and cathedrals, and the mosques of Islam, for instance, were built with this consciousness, with the effect of creating a sacred and inspiring atmosphere not only within the buildings but in the land all around.

Looking at the basic design of a cathedral in the light of this knowledge, it can be clearly seen that the cathedral actually represents the human body and its energy system. As figure 33 shows, the classic cathedral has the shape of the human being lying on the ground on his or her back, with outstretched arms, looking upward toward heaven. Like the human body, it consists of three main components—a chancel, a nave and a central crossing—representing respectively the head, the abdomen, and the chest.

Within the head area (the chancel), the throat is represented by the choir, and the brow by the presbytery where the bishop's chair, or *cathedra*, is set up. The crown chakra is the sanctuary where the high altar stands. Where there is an apse, this represents the dome of the head. A screen, originally the *pulpitum* from where the Word of God was preached, separates the head from the chest area.

The place where the transepts cross the nave (the central crossing) at the chest area is the most important part of any cathedral or church; in the archetypal cathedral it contains the heart center. The central tower, lantern, or dome, supported on four great arches, is placed over this crossing, so that if you were to stand in its center you would be in the heart of a Cosmic Cross, with one arm of the cross stretching to the east, one to the west, one to the south, one to the north, with the tower soaring above into the heavens, and the foundations beneath going deep into the earth. The Cosmic Cross represents the Cosmos itself.

Within the abdomen (the nave) are contained the three lower chakras. In the original cathedrals there was normally a nave altar for the general public at the eastern end of the solar plexus chakra area, with a rood screen behind it separating the nave from the heart of the cathedral. The rood screen represents the diaphragm between the abdomen and chest, just as the *pulpitum* or chancel screen signifies the second diaphragm which separates the chest from the head. Tradition refers to these as the veils of the temple. The ordinary members of the congregation sat in the abdomen area, and the higher chakras—the heart area and above—were reserved for the clergy and monks, the latter usually being located in the head or chancel of the cathedral.

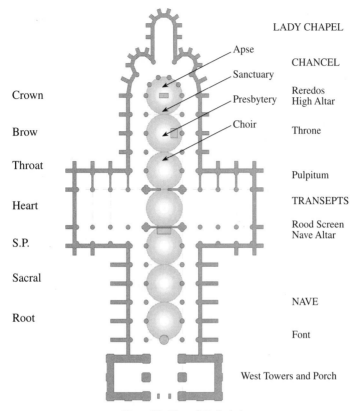

LADY CHAPEL

Apse

CHANCEL

Sanctuary

Crown · Presbytery · Reredos
High Altar

Brow · Choir · Throne

Throat

Pulpitum

Heart

TRANSEPTS

S.P. · Rood Screen
Nave Altar

Sacral

NAVE

Root

Font

West Towers and Porch

Figure 33. Plan of Cathedral.

The font at the west end normally lies in the root chakra of the cathedral, although sometimes it is to be found in the sacral chakra area. (In countries such as Denmark, it is usually in the heart area, for different reasons.) The element that fills the font is water, which symbolizes the coiled earth energy, waiting to be aroused and drawn up the spine of the church. The stone font and the water within it represent the *water* and *earth* of Biblical tradition. Balancing this, at the crown chakra, the candle-lit high altar with its ever-burning flame, its cross and its incense, represent the spiritual energy—the *fire* and *air*, or fiery breath, of Biblical tradition. These polarities, signifying the spirit of God and the waters of the Universe, are essential to the life of the cathedral: for creation occurs when the spirit of God moves upon the face of the waters.

The full design of a cathedral shows more than this: it is an architectural representation of the same truth that is depicted in the icons of the Mother Mary with her Christ child. Mary sits with the Christ child on her lap, supporting the child; and the child's head lies at the heart of his mother. This emblem of a profound truth forms the architectural plan of the cathedral, which has an inner and an outer church. The inner church, as already described, represents the Christ child. The outer church, formed by the side aisles, the ambulatory, the twin west towers and the Lady Chapel in the east, symbolizes the divine Mother, whose head is represented by the Lady Chapel and whose legs are portrayed by the western towers. There is often a cross (or monument of some kind) placed outside the west door, in the center of the entry court, which marks the root chakra of the Mother (See Plate 4, page 46.)

Entering a church or cathedral at the west end, you will find yourself naturally drawn toward the east end, as if by a magnet, just as the earth energies are naturally stirred by the rays of spiritual energy and drawn up the spine. Christian allegory, itself adopted from earlier wisdom teachings, explains this attraction as being that of the spear of the Great Fisherman (i.e. the Christ) who fishes us out of the waters of life and into the air and fire (i.e. fiery breath) of the Holy Spirit. The Fisherman story is equivalent to the St. George allegory. Every disciple is symbolized as a fish, the fish being an alternative form of the dragon. The bishop, who is both a disciple and also a representative of the Christ, dresses up in a symbolic way so as to portray both a fish and the fisherman; his miter, for instance, represents a fish head, while his staff is a composite symbol of a shepherd's crook and a fisherman's spear. The walk up the nave is a journey up the spine of the church, through each of the chakras, culminating at the crown chakra with holy communion or union with the light. Making this journey with the conscious awareness of its deeper meaning can have a powerful spiritual effect.

When the congregation moves through a church up the central aisle to the high altar and back down the side aisles, in a procession such as at mass or holy communion, they are following the flow of earth energy through the chakras and down again on each side, helping to create and enhance the sparkling fountain of life and celestial form of the church. Moreover, by assisting this process in the church they also stimulate the process in themselves.

TOWNSCAPES

Towns, even cities, can be (and have been in the past) designed as large-scale temples, containing complete chakra systems. When done with full consciousness the town chakras have been carefully placed in the natural environment, coinciding with chakras naturally occurring in the landscape. There are many examples all over the world where key buildings, such as temples, palaces, market places, government buildings, and the like, have been sited on appropriate energy points that are conducive to the type of activity taking place in the building. In addition the buildings themselves were often constructed according to cosmic principles and in ways to enhance the type of chakric energy.

The harmonious and energetic layout of a town can also occur naturally, growing organically with its chakra system, when its inhabitants are allowed to build intuitively, with care and inspiration, and there are many examples of this. The axis or spine of a town does not have to follow a straight line, but it is vitally important that polarities exist. The greater the polarity, the more energized the place can be—for instance, when the head area is raised on a hill and the root area is low-lying, such as in a valley, and associated with water, whether a lake, river or the sea.

In an ideal townscape, the heart area should be a center of peace, harmony, and beauty, reflecting the function of the heart. They should be places where people naturally like to go, to be peaceful, to meet each other quietly and to enjoy the beauty. It helps to have a fountain, sculpture, cross, or tree in the center, providing both a central focus and the vertical element, to form the three-dimensional cosmic cross (as in the central crossing and tower of a cathedral). A fountain is especially good, as it cleanses the atmosphere and imitates the natural upward movement of earth energy that creates the celestial body and aura.

Churches can be placed in any chakra of the town, but the positions traditionally used most often are the heart, throat, brow, crown, and root areas.

The throat area, the center of intelligence and of speaking and listening, is a very good position for education and culture, and therefore for schools, theaters, concert halls, and the like. Schools for younger children are best placed in the area of the throat next to the heart, while the part of the throat chakra approaching the brow is appropriate for colleges, universities, libraries, and places of higher education. Administrative buildings function very well in the brow chakra area, as do offices, town halls, and so on. It is also good for universities and research work.

Castles used to be built on brow chakras, to make use of the dominating, controlling energy that the brow chakra tends to have.

Markets and shopping areas, the great centers of commerce and trade, function best in the solar plexus area; so do restaurants, pubs, and other eating places. The solar plexus center benefits if it includes a market cross or similar structure as a focal point, with an area around it for social gatherings and activities. Industries and workshops function well in the sacral chakra (as also do red light areas), while activities involving distribution and storage naturally belong to the root chakra area.

EDINBURGH'S ROYAL MILE

A good example of a townscape temple is Edinburgh's Royal Mile, stretching along the High Street which rises from east to west, from Canongate near Holyrood Park to Edinburgh Castle perched on its rock. (See figure 34, page 89.) The old city was built along this road, and the streets that cross it help to delineate the chakra areas. (Plate 5, page 47.)

The Palace of Holyrood lies on the energy center just outside the chakra system (equivalent in function to the cross that stands outside the west door of a cathedral). As you set out on the mile-long walk from the palace of Holyrood toward Edinburgh Castle, you come first to Canon Gate, the root chakra, originally the gate into the old city. The sacral area starts where St. Mary's Street crosses the High Street. It used to be Edinburgh's red light area! Nowadays it includes the Museum of Childhood. The solar plexus area starts at North and South Bridge Streets; here, appropriately, the majority of shops are found.

At the heart chakra lie St. Giles' Cathedral and Parliament House. (Plate 6, page 48.) Here the Heart of Lothian, a heart-shaped stone, is actually set in the pavement. Above it we go through the area of the throat chakra, which includes the Traverse Theater. The brow is on the first part of the Castle Rock, just below the Castle; it includes a perfectly positioned *Camera Obscura*, through which you can see the whole of Edinburgh, and it is in the adjoining open space in front of the castle that the grand visual display of the Edinburgh Tattoo takes place each year.

The Castle, higher still, is at the crown chakra—and *is* the crown of Edinburgh. It is capped by St. Margaret's Chapel, Edinburgh's oldest building, which has a wonderful, peaceful atmosphere. Interestingly, Margaret means "pearl" and the "pearl of great price" traditionally capped the royal crown. (See Plate 7, page 48.)

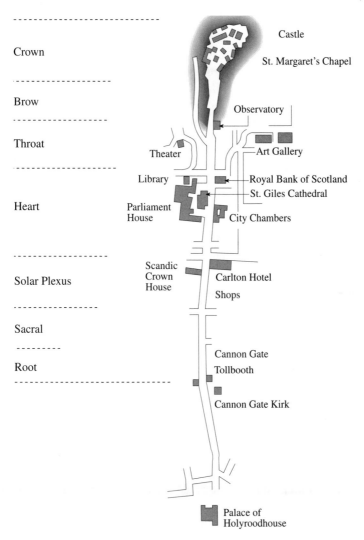

Figure 34. Edinburgh Royal Mile Townscape Temple.

STEIN-AM-RHEIN

Another good example of a medieval townscape complete with chakras, well-preserved and exceptionally beautiful, is Stein-am-Rhein on the banks of the High Rhine. Unlike Edinburgh, its chakric system does not stretch from a low valley to the crown of a hill. Instead the chakric system of this pretty town is laid out alongside the river, on the flat, with the Rhine flowing from east to west along the town's southern side and a moat originally protecting the town walls on the landward sides. (See Plate 8, page 49.)

The town's overall design is very interesting and special. Whereas Edinburgh is laid out with its Royal Mile snaking its way up the hillside, imitating the course of the dragon energy, Stein-am-Rhein is designed to show the "Y" pattern that is the age-old sign of surrender and illumination. That is to say, its main streets are laid out in the form of the hero crucified on the cross, with his arms raised to form, with his body, the letter "Y"—the same sign that is to be found carved in the rock of the Externsteine, even to the similarity of the head tilted to the side, toward the right shoulder, signifying the moment of death and illumination.

This is not a unique layout, for there are other places with this design, but they are not common. It marks out the town as being a place out of the ordinary; and maybe a notion of its secret lies in its name, *Steine*. For a stone to give its name to a town, it must have been a special stone, a marker of some significance. Stones have traditionally been used as markers of special places, as altar stones and standing stones, and as "pillow stones" erected on a sacred site where meaningful dreams or visions have occurred. Stones erected in this way, on special energy spots, help to focus rays of spiritual energy from the cosmos upon the Earth, piercing the dragon energy of the Earth at the key chakras in the landscape so that transformation and transmutation can take place. One of the reasons why the hierophants of the mystery schools were called "Stones" is because this is exactly what they were able to do, from a human point of view.

The town's position in the High Rhine landscape temple is indeed significant, for the town lies in the solar plexus chakra of the High Rhine. (See figure 35.) The solar plexus is the place of crucifixion of the lower ego or dragon-self, as is shown by the similar position of the crucified man on the solar plexus rock of the Externsteine, and of the crucifix on the rood screen in a cathedral. In other words, the design of the town's main streets and chakric system is exactly appropriate as a symbol of its position in the High Rhine landscape temple, whose root chakra is centered on the Isle of Reichenau and whose crown is marked by the Rhine Falls.

Crown

Brow

Throat

Heart

Solar Plexus

Sacral

Root

Church

Library
Rose House

Town Hall

Town Square
Fountain

Gatehouse

Figure 35. Stein-am-Rhein Townscape Temple.

The chakric system of Stein-am-Rhein begins with the town's western gateway, with the root chakra located immediately within the gateway at the start of the Unterstadt. This western gateway is equivalent to the western doorway of a cathedral, with the head of the town laid out to the east.

The spine of the town curves eastward subtly like a serpent, similar to the artistic depictions of Jesus on the cross, or of the Gnostic serpent on the cross. Side streets join the spinal route at key intervals, two of them marking the change from one chakra to the next. Where the Unterstadt gives way to the Rathausplatz, the solar plexus chakra and the main shops begin, all highly decorated with symbolic wall paintings and carvings. Some of the symbols match in a remarkable way the actual chakra of the town that their building is in. The Rathausplatz forms the old market place, bordered with shops, cafés and restaurants.

The heart chakra is located in the eastern half of the Rathausplatz. A fine fountain with a St. George and Dragon sculpture surmounting it marks the divide between the solar plexus and the heart area. Again, following the ancient wisdom tradition, the dragon is depicted being slain in the higher part of the solar plexus chakra of the town, at the "veil" which leads into the heart.

At the eastern end of the Rathausplatz is the Town Hall (Rathaus). At this point the two main side streets come into the heart of the town from the north and the south, the former via the north gate of the town and the latter via a bridge over the Rhine. Meeting in the heart, in the Rathausplatz, they form two arms of the town's cosmic cross. Eastward, the main axis of the town divides into two streets, one passing to the south of the Town Hall, the other to the north. These two streets, the Chirchhofplatz and Oberstraße, form the two raised arms of the town's mystery figure.

Immediately behind the Town Hall, on its east side, is the town library, located beneficially in the throat chakra of the town. Continuing further east, the Chirchhofplatz leads to the ancient church and convent of St. George, in the area of the brow chakra, but associated with the left arm of the town's symbolic pattern. Balancing the Church of St. George, and associated with the right arm and throat chakra of the town, is a remarkable building in the Oberstraße which was once the Guildhouse of the traders, and which portrays the symbols of the Rosicrucians; that is to say, it represents the esoteric counterpart to the clergy's church of St. George, for St. George is the Christian Rose Cross Knight. The Guildhouse is called the Zunfthaus zur Rosen, and its outside wall, facing the street, has a remarkable painting of Christian Rosencreutz on it. Rosencreutz is accompanied by two companions, depicted in a stance that indicates the symbolism of the "Triple A"—an ancient sign of the esoteric societies and mystery schools dating back at least as far as Ancient Egypt.

The Church of St. George associated with the brow chakra and left arm, and the Guildhouse of Christian Rosencreutz associated with the throat chakra and right arm, is entirely appropriate according to traditional symbolism, for the true Rosicrucians are like prophets, inspired and providing inspiration by revealing the inner teachings of the ever-living Christ, the Word, while the clerical and priestly Church deals principally with organizing and presenting the written form of those teachings to the general public. They are like the Sun and the Moon to each other, although, of course, each has something of the other as well, manifesting what the Chinese refer to as the *yin-yang* principle. This layout of the town demonstrates that these buildings were clearly placed in their positions by conscious design.

The east gate of the town is now destroyed, and this eastern part of the town, in the crown chakra, is the only part which is a little sad and not at the moment worthy of its position.

BERLIN

Scotland's capital, Edinburgh, still preserves its original medieval town with its complete chakric system in the heart of the modern city. Germany's capital, Berlin, however, is an example of a city whose medieval heart is now largely destroyed, but which has grown a later, enlarged chakric system that incorporates the vestiges of the old town in its heart. (See figure 36, page 94.) For various reasons part of this later chakric system is very clear and seemingly laid out deliberately, while the part containing the lower chakras is obscured. The spine of the chakric system lies alongside the River Spree, with the river forming a meandering spine adjacent to and complementing the straight line of the man-made axis of the city.

The heart of Berlin is formed by the area of the old medieval town, particularly the region stretching westward from the 19th-century Red Town Hall (Rotes Rathaus), Marx-Engels Forum, and the Romanesque-Gothic Church of St. Nicholas (Nikolaikirche) on the east bank of the River Spree, to include the whole of the world-famed Museum Island (Museumsinsel) and the Marx-Engels Platz on the site of the old Town Palace (Stadtschloss), the modern Palace of the Republic (Palast der Republik) and the Berlin Cathedral (Dome), all of which are on an island surrounded by the waters of the Spree. (See Plate 9, page 49.)

From this great heart-center the famous lime avenue, Unter den Linden, is dramatically laid out east-west to form the axis of the city, reaching from the heart center through the higher chakras, and eventually shooting through the crown to become the Bismarckstraße and Heerstraße, powerfully channelling the earth energy of the city from east to

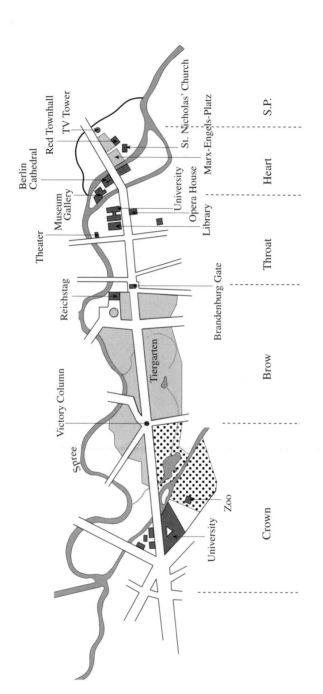

Figure 36. Berlin Townscape Temple.

west (following the flow of the river), and the spiritual energy into the city center from west to east. The city's heart center, on its island, plays its part by catching the water energy of the river (associated with nature's dragon or earth energy) and channelling it up the Unter den Linden toward the crown chakra and out to the west.

Berlin's throat chakra lies each side of the Unter den Linden, containing the National Library (Deutsche Staatsbibliothek), the Humboldt University (Humbolt-Universität), St. Hedwig's Cathedral (St. Hedwigs-Kathedrale), the Opera House (Deutsche Staatsoper), the Comic Opera (Komishe Oper), plus other museums, libraries and theaters.

The Unter den Linden leads to the Pariser Platz, in which stands the famous Brandenburg Gate (Brandenburger Tor), the emblem of Berlin. Nearby is the old Reichstag Building (Reichstagsgebäudel) in the Platz der Republik, and the modern Congress Hall (Kongresshalle). This is the area of the brow chakra—the place where policies are discussed, decisions are made, and instructions given. It is interesting that it was across the Pariser Platz that the division of Berlin into East and West was made, cutting right through the eye of the city—the command center.

Continuing further west, the Unter den Linden Avenue becomes the great avenue known as the Straße des 17 Juni, traversing straight as an arrow through the Tiergarten to the Ernst-Reuter Platz, and then becoming the Bismarckstraße. This Tiergarten, with its meandering waterways and lakes, is a joyful expression of the brow and crown chakras, culminating at the west end of the Tiergarten with the University of Technology (Technische Universität) and Zoological Garden (Zoologischer Garten) in the crown.

The Bismarckstraße carries the axis of the city even further west, crossing the city's western autobahn and distributing its "fountain" of energy to the Charlottenburg district and to whatever else might lie in the west.

WASHINGTON, DC

Washington, DC, the capital of the United States of America, contains a remarkable city center, delightfully laid out and graced with beautiful buildings. Designed, evolved, and built on land that was a mixture of swamp and underbrush just two centuries ago, during the turbulent formative period of the United States, it makes a fitting tribute to the architects, leaders and people of the United States. Built to house the focal centers of the nation's three branches of government—executive, legislative and judicial—the plan of the city center incorporates these three as the President's White House, the Capitol and the Supreme Court, linked together by the landscaped Mall and a network of roads. (See figure 37, page 97.)

The original design by the French engineer, Pierre Charles L'Enfant, has been modified and enlarged over time, but the original concept can still be seen. Indeed, the modifications have allowed a clear chakra system to emerge, with the Mall forming its east-west spine. In terms of the whole city, this governmental city center forms a head chakra, which is indeed fitting for its purpose, for both the government of the city as well as of the whole nation. The type of buildings in this city center, their purpose and chakric relationship to each other, reflect the fact that it is a governmental center, the "head" of the nation.

The plan of the city center is based on Jenkins' Hill, the area's highest elevation, on which is built the Capitol, home of Congress. From the steps and terraces of the Capitol, the grand Mall runs westward toward the Potomac River, where it culminates with the memorial to Abraham Lincoln. This memorial is in the style of a flat-roofed Greek Doric temple, a testament in stone to the sixteenth President of the United States of America, who preserved the Union and, with it, the ideal of an enduring and democratic republic. The great statue of Lincoln within the temple, seated on his massive chair, looks powerfully to the east, toward the Capitol. This statue and memorial, situated on the bank of the river, form a strong and suitable root chakra, architecturally and symbolically, to balance the crown chakra that is represented by the domed Capitol on its hill. (See Plates 10–13, pages 50–51.)

Between the Capitol and the Lincoln Memorial is stretched the Mall, the spine of the townscape, comprising a two-mile sweep of grass, trees, and water. Two great reflecting pools, one beneath Capitol Hill and the other in front of the Lincoln Memorial, are the main elements of its formalized water display. By the side of the long pool in the west that reflects the Lincoln Memorial is a lake, and these two together, lake and pool, both situated in the western part of the Mall known as Constitution Gardens, form a good focus of the sacral and solar plexus chakras of the Mall. The State and Interior Departments, and the Federal Reserve buildings, are suitably associated with this area, lining the north side of Constitution Gardens.

At the heart of the Mall stands a soaring obelisk, 555.5 feet (168 meters) high, built of marble as a memorial to George Washington, the first

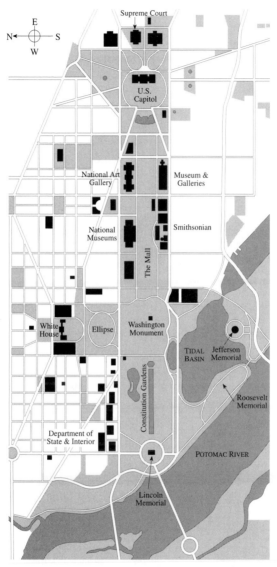

Figure 37. Washington, DC Townscape Temple.

President, who fought for and presided over the birth of the nation. Fittingly, the monument stands in the heart chakra of the townscape, the place of spiritual birth. Crossing this heart area, like the transepts of a cathedral, is a north-south extension of the Mall. As in a cathedral, the Mall, the "transepts," and the obelisk form the symbol of a three-dimensional cosmic cross. The northern "transept" comprises the White House in its garden, with the park known as the Ellipse laid out in front of it. The southern "transept" is mainly composed of water, the Tidal Basin, on the southern shore of which is situated the Jefferson Memorial, commemorating the third President and principal author of the Declaration of Independence. (See Plate 14, page 52.)

The domed Pantheon-style classical memorial to Thomas Jefferson looks northward over the Tidal Basin to the Washington Monument and beyond to the White House, while the frontage of the White House looks southward over the lawns and trees of the Ellipse to the great obelisk and the Jefferson Memorial. Not far from the latter is the recently completed (1997) massive granite and water memorial to Theodore Roosevelt, also flanking the Tidal Basin. Making a suitable polarity to each other, the memorials to these two dead Presidents are on the left-hand side of the townscape, and associated with water, while the house of the living President is on the right-hand side, built on high ground. Although not always to be found like this in the landscape, nor necessary, this arrangement does neatly reflect the traditional idea which associates wisdom with the right and with fire, and understanding (which stands under wisdom) with the left and with water. Also related with this in traditional symbolism is the association of the right with life and the left with death.

East of the Washington Monument, the Mall is lined on either side with museums and art galleries, all mainly founded through philanthropic donations, including the world-famous Smithsonian Institute and the National Gallery of Art. This eastern part of the Mall culminates in the east at the foot of the Capitol hill with the curved reflecting pool of the Capitol. The whole of this eastern stretch of the Mall, although the longest part, forms the throat chakra of the townscape, its buildings being a fine manifestation of the kind of cultural activities that thrive in throat chakra energies.

Likewise, the white marble and sandstone Capitol on its hill is entirely suited to the natural functions of a brow and crown chakra, its steps leading up to terraces with magnificent views along the Mall and other avenues which radiate from the Capitol. The division of the Capitol building into two wings on either side of the central domed hall, to accommodate the functions of House and Senate, is expressive of the two hemispheres of the brain, the House of Representatives being associated with the left-hand hemisphere (south wing) and the Senate with the right-hand hemisphere (north wing). The Supreme Court, which once was accommodated in the Capitol building, is now housed in a nearby building on Jenkins Hill.

The grand Dome, which rises high above the Capitol's central hall, forms a striking visual manifestation of the crown chakra of the city center. Itself crowned with a great bronze statue of Freedom, it declares the inspirational ideal and aspirational goal of the whole nation.

FIVE

Natural Landscape Forms

All are but parts of one stupendous whole,
Whose body nature is and God the soul.
—ALEXANDER POPE

As we well know, human beings have a major impact upon the natural
environment, and we seem to be able to do whatever we like, given the appropriate technology; but many people simply do not realize the power and
influence, often subtle, that the natural environment has on us, nor do they
recognize nature's intelligence. Nature's places tend to mold us to their nature, rather than the other way around. If we were to pause and reflect on
this, we might realize what Alexander Pope realized, and be humble, and
discover that we each have our place as well as our role to play.

Places that are right for us, like roles, can also change with time, as we
evolve and follow our chosen paths in life. To know how to do the right
thing in the right place at the right time, etc., is the key to the practical science of living in harmony both in and with our world. The world is nature's architecture. It is made for us and our fellow creatures, as a gift. If we
learn to use it rightly, to care for it and to enhance it appropriately, it helps
us immeasurably, for the world is the form of a living, intelligent being. It
is possible to develop a dialogue with the world, and to become partners
with it in the art of living. This is a primary aim of Zoence.

LANDSCAPE TEMPLES

The whole planet is a temple in its own right—a well-ordered form of energy, vibrant with life and consciousness, with its own greater and lesser chakras focusing the life forces and intelligence of the planet according to a grand design.

As in the human body, there are areas of the landscape that show all the chakras and have an energy structure similar to that underlying the physical body. In Zoence these are known as landscape temples. There are both small and large ones, the small ones lying within the larger. Every chakra of a large landscape temple is, itself, a smaller temple with its own set of chakras—microcosms within macrocosms.

Since landscape temples may be spread out across the land for miles, this is not always an easy concept to grasp. However, by using your intuition together with your ordinary senses, you can become aware of areas of landscape that are working as temples. The first features to look for are a sense of polarity and a flow of energy between the poles (perhaps as a river, or a way up a hillside from its base to its crown, etc.). Look, too, for the heart area. If the landscape temple is healthy and well-balanced, the heart will be a focal point of harmony and peace. If the energy pattern really exists, and you find a good attunement with the spirit of the place, the rest will then probably unfold for you.

THE EXTERNSTEINE

One fascinating and famous example of a natural temple in the landscape is the Externsteine, a monumental formation of rocks located in the Teutoburg Forest near Detmold in northern Germany. Carved out by natural forces under angelic (i.e., spiritual) direction, these extraordinary rock formations express the chakric system in a dramatic way. (See Plates 15 and 16, pages 52, 53.)

The name *Externsteine* means "Dragon Stones," and these rocks which emerge out of the northwestern end of a long hill ridge do, indeed, give the appearance of a dragon in the landscape, with a rocky armored body and long tail, sliding out of the hillside of the Wiembecke valley in order to drink its water. (See figure 38.)

The Externsteine has been a major center of attraction and human occupation for thousands of years, and for a large part of this time it has been a religious center of some sort, pre-Christian and Christian. The

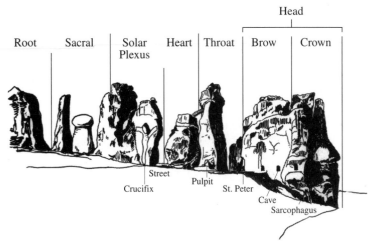

Figure 38. The Externsteine Landscape Temple.

place is now looked after by the forest authorities of the Landesverband Lippe, and open to be enjoyed by all.

The best view of the Externsteine is as one walks from the main carpark and toilet area toward the rocks. As you emerge from the woods, you are able to see the complete expanse of the rocks; and if you look carefully, with an intuitive, perceptive eye, you will be able to recognize the chakric pattern stamped in the rocks, together with various symbolic forms associated with those chakras. Some of the symbolic forms are natural and some have been fashioned by people, enhancing the natural features. From this it is quite clear that many people have previously recognized the chakric system in the rocks, and have used the rocks accordingly, as a temple.

It is probably easiest to begin looking for the chakras at the root of the Externsteine chakric system, where the dragon's rocky body emerges from the forest at the top end of the dragon's buried tail. One huge rock marks the root chakra, where the rocky body of the dragon emerges from the wooded hillside out into the open, anchoring the Externsteine to the earth with power and strength. The next group of rocks show quite clearly the symbol of an erect phallus within a vagina, a powerful emblem of the sacral chakra.

The third set of rocks, a massive structure, marks the solar plexus chakra. The solar plexus is the seat of the lower ego, where most of the desires of the ordinary personality tend to be focused. It is this ego which needs to "die," so that its nature can be transformed into the higher nature that is heart-centered and spiritually aware. The Ancient Egyptians and later societies identified the liver with this seat of the lower ego, and the heart as the throne of the higher ego, or soul.

In Church tradition, the ego-sacrifice is represented by the crucifix, which is placed on the rood screen of an abbey or cathedral, so that it hangs over the nave altar. Outlined on the side of the Externsteine's solar plexus rock, on that part of the rock corresponding in position to the nave altar in a cathedral, is a giant representation of a crucified man, either Baldur or Jesus. This outline is mostly natural, created by cracks in the rock, but enhanced by human beings to make the features clearer, including a hole in the lower right chest to represent the place where the spear pierced the liver of Jesus.

Between this solar plexus rock and the adjacent heart rock is a gap or "Arch" through which the Reichstraße 1 (Aachen–Paderborn–Hameln–Königsberg) once passed, which in 1813 replaced the course of the ancient trade route that originally lay lower down in the Wiembecke Valley and which previously had passed around (*i.e.* in front of) the head of the Externsteine. This gap used by the Reichstraße creates a natural "veil" or "diaphragm" between the lower and higher chakras of the Externsteine.

The heart chakra rock is a smaller rock than the others, lying the other side of the Reichstraße gap. It used to have a small chapel at the top, cut out of the living rock, but this has long been destroyed and only the foundations remain. Carved out of the sides of this heart rock is a winding staircase leading to the top of the rock, where a bridge leaps over another, thinner gap.

This bridge leads to the upper part of the adjacent throat chakra rock, where most of the original rock-cut chamber still remains, with one side and part of the roof having fallen away. This chamber has a small circular window carved through the eastern wall of the rock, above an altar, and facing it on the west wall of the chamber is a carved recess in which a man can stand, with two finger-holds each side to fix his position. From this position a six-foot person can see the Sun rise over a sacred hill on the horizon at the Summer Solstice.

The final and largest group of rocks incorporates both the head chakras—brow and crown. Like a skull, the head rock is hollowed out in part to form a cavern, man-made, with an original entrance from the throat area guarded by a carving of St. Peter with the keys. The apostle Simon Peter is associated with the throat, as his role was as the hierophant and speaker for the zodiacal circle of Jesus' apostles, and the representative of faith, the intuitive love that is the foundation of the initiatic cycle. His two names, Simon Peter, signify the function of the throat, meaning "he who hears" and "the revealer (or speaker)" respectively. He is the gatekeeper who opens the door of the heart to the mind, so that the light may be seen—the gatekeeper corresponding to the Taurus Cherub.

The side of the brow chakra rock has a highly detailed carving on it representing Jesus being taken down from the cross so that his body could be entombed. It is an appropriate picture to display outside the Golgotha-type cavern (*Golgotha* means "skull") that lies hidden in the rock behind the carving. It is also the first Christian monumental sculpture of its kind, and probably the most important example in the whole of northwest Europe.

Lower down the side of the head rock is an actual tomb—a rock-cut sarcophagus. High above, on the top of the brow chakra rock, is a platform where the visitor can, appropriately, gain a good view over the surrounding landscape, looking up and down the Wiembecke Valley. On the summit of the very end rock, overlooking the newly created lake in the valley, is the crown of the Externsteine, where some people believe that a cross, or *Irminsul*, was once erected.

The Externsteine is, itself, part of several other larger landscape temples, one of which lies between the Externsteine and the great national monument, Hermannsdenkmal, on the Grotenburg, seven kilometers to the northeast. Herman is portrayed like a gigantic St. Michael figure, waving his sword high above the crown of a hill which itself is the crown of this larger landscape temple. The Externsteine is its natural polarity, being the Earth-dragon lurking in its root chakra lair.

THE LANDSCAPE TEMPLE
OF LONDON AND THE THAMES

This important landscape temple stretches from the Chiltern Hills to Greenwich, its spine following the route of the River Thames. The gateway to the temple is at Goring, where the river first enters the Chiltern Hills. The gateway is marked by a hill on each side, like the two pillars of a gate, and is the point where the ancient trackway of the Celts and Romans crosses the Thames. Its "mother" root chakra, which

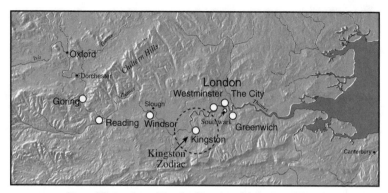

Figure 39. Landscape Temple of London and the River Thames.
From Mountain High Maps® Copyright © 1993 Digital Wisdom, Inc.
Used by permission.

is located several miles upriver, outside the gateway, is at Dorchester-on-Thames, a place of great geomantic importance where the parent rivers of the Thames—the Isis and the Thame—have their confluence. (See figure 39, above.)

The root chakra of the London-Thames landscape temple occupies the river valley through the Chilterns as far as the industrial area of Reading, where the sacral chakra begins. Beyond Reading the river breaks out into the open plain, curving around the sacral area via Henley, Marlow, and Maidenhead, with a central power point at Knowl Hill. This is a particularly beautiful part of the Thames, and is very feminine and womb-like.

At Windsor we find the solar plexus chakra, the center of personal power and ego; it is entirely appropriate that Windsor Castle is the personal family seat of the present British Royal Family. They are following an old tradition, for Windsor is believed to have been the personal seat of King Arthur and the home of the Round Table. (Arthur's royal seat was at Westminster.) The Knights of the Garter, who have their headquarters and royal chapel at Windsor Castle, and whose special emblem is St. George and the Dragon, were founded as a revival of the Arthurian tradition.

After Windsor and Staines, we enter Chertsey through the equivalent of the diaphragm, the veil protecting the heart center. The heart itself is at Kingston-upon-Thames, which is the center of a landscape zodiac stretching from Chertsey, on one side, to Putney, on the other. (Landscape zodiacs show the energy pattern of the zodiac, "the circle of creatures," manifested naturally in the landscape as if imprinted from the cosmos and, when recognized, enhanced and named by human beings. They are usually found at heart centers, and are the source of the Round Table stories—the zodiac being the Round Table. The zodiac surrounding the heart center is also the origin of the story of the birth of Christ in the cave surrounded by the animals—the cave where the light of love is born being the heart chakra.)

All the way along the Thames one part of each chakra lies on one side and one on the other. The two parts have slightly different characteristics, which become particularly marked as we enter London. Leaving the Kingston zodiac, the river enters the throat chakra through Chelsea, on one side, and Battersea, on the other. Battersea has its recently built Peace Pagoda and garden, enhancing an otherwise neglected area. The throat chakra ends at Westminster and Lambeth. Thorney Isle, upon which Westminster stands, marks a higher part of the throat area, representing the alta major chakra: hence its vital importance for the British monarchy and Parliament.

The brow area is occupied by the City of London, on one side, and Bankside (the South Bank), on the other. In the center of the City is St. Paul's Cathedral, while the Tower of London stands on its east end, with all the famous banks and offices of London's financial center in between. The association of ravens with the Tower is interesting, since clairvoyants see the fully developed brow chakra as having two wings, known as raven's wings. Moreover, the raven is an emblem of the great god Bran, whose head is supposedly buried beneath the Tower, protecting London. The activities of the City are highly appropriate for the brow chakra, though the energy has become rather over-rigid. This rigidity is somewhat counteracted by the imaginative cultural and artistic activities of Bankside where, for instance, the newly built Shakespeare Globe Theatre stands in pride of place next door to the old Bankside power station, which is in the process of becoming the new Tate Gallery.

The crown is represented by the Isle of Dogs ("Docks") and Greenwich, with another strong contrast between the two sides. The Isle of Dogs was once the port from which ships went out into all parts of the world, imitating, in a rather materialistic way, the outpouring of energy from the crown chakra to the Universe. But it was also once the gate through which some wisdom was sent from Britain to other parts of the world, and by which much wisdom was brought back into Britain. Now it no longer has this same role, as the docks are dismantled and the area is in the process of redevelopment.

Greenwich, on the southern side of the river, is a perfect crown chakra site, a place of peace and beauty which people love to visit. Besides a lovely park, and the elegant architecture of the Royal Naval College and the National Maritime Museum (originally built as a hospital), Greenwich also includes, appropriately, the Greenwich Meridian, marking the basic longitude and time meridian for the whole world, and the famous Observatory. Nearby is the site on which the Millennium Dome is being built, in which will repose the giant Mother and Child sculpture—a highly appropriate symbol for the crown of the London-Thames landscape temple and mythos of Britain.

THE "IROQUOIS" LANDSCAPE TEMPLE

A fascinating example of a landscape temple in North America that was at one time recognized, used, and enhanced by human beings, is that territory which now comprises the major part of New York State, especially the northern and western areas. This landscape, which was once the home of the Iroquois tribes who formed the famous League of Five Nations, stretches from Niagara Falls in the west to the Adirondack Mountains in the east. The territory is bordered on the north by Lake Ontario and the St. Lawrence River, and on the south by the Allegheny and Catskill Mountains.

This landscape is particularly interesting as the birthplace and homeland of a confederacy of nations who, having previously been at war with each other, came together in peace under a remarkable political constitution which, to some extent, formed a model for both the Constitution of the United States and the Constitution of the United Nations. Moreover, it provided equal rights in law for women, together with unique responsibilities and privileges, long before the women of the European settlers, or European women themselves, ever obtained similar rights.

When "the Great Peace," the Confederacy of the Iroquois, was formed by the Peacemaker Deganawida and his spokesman Hiawatha, the five Iroquoian nations that constituted the initial League were already living in this landscape. These five tribes (from west to east) were the Seneca, the Cayuga, the Onondaga, the Oneida and the Mohawk. The Seneca were the westernmost tribe, whose territory eventually reached as far as the Niagara Falls and Lake Erie. The Mohawk formed the easternmost tribe, whose tribal lands reached to the Hudson River in the east and the St. Lawrence River in the north, and included not only the Adirondacks but also the strategically important Mohawk Valley, one of the two gateways and the only water route through the "Endless Mountains" (the Appalachian chain). The Onondaga were the middle tribe of the five, centered on their sacred lake where now the city of Syracuse lies.

One of the principal features of the Iroquoian landscape is the Finger Lakes—long stretches of water formed from northward-flowing streams which drain the glaciated valleys of the Allegheny Mountains into Lake Ontario. Iroquoian legend describes these lakes as having been made by the hand of the Great God Manitou, who formed them as he was pushing the heavenly Paradise down onto Earth in order to create the Iroquoian paradise. In doing this, Manitou's hand slipped and six lakes were formed instead of five. The three easternmost Finger Lakes— Canandaigua, Keuka, and Seneca—lay in the Seneca tribal land. The longest lake, Lake Cayuga, lay in the territory of the Cayuga nation, and the two easternmost lakes, Owasco and Skaneateles, belonged to the Onondagas. The Onondagas also had their central lake, Lake Onondaga, while the Oneidas were blessed with the large, rounded and beautiful Lake Oneida further to the east.

The League of the Five Nations was formed on the pattern of the Iroquoian longhouse, and the Iroquoian name for the confederacy was *Ko-no-shi-oni,* meaning "the (Great) Long House." The elm bark longhouse was the main dwelling of the Iroquois, each one accommodating up to ten families. Every family would share a fire with another family, one on one side of the longhouse and the other on the opposite side. The ideal longhouse would therefore have five fires down its center and ten "firesides" or family units.

The longhouses were oriented east-west, each with a door to the east and another to the west. The firesides nearest each door were termed the keepers of the east door or west door respectively. The central fire was the heart fire and the families tending it were the keepers of this heart fire and the "firekeepers" generally of the longhouse (*i.e.* the "judges" in any deliberation). The firesides associated with the in-between fires were related symbolically to the other main directions, the fire to the east of the central fire being associated with the north, and the fire to the west of the central fire being associated with the south.

This longhouse cosmology was transferred as a symbolic image to the whole League of Five Nations and its combined territory, so that the Mohawks became the Keepers of the East Door, the Senecas became the Keepers of the West Door, the Oneida became the guardians of the northern "walls," and the Cayuga became the guardians of the southern "walls." Of these, the Mohawks came first in precedence. The Onondagas were appointed the Firekeepers (or judges) in the middle, responsible for keeping the central fire, emblem of the League's heart, and presiding over all meetings of the Council.

This cosmology describes both the circle of the horizon with its four main directions and center, and also a chakric system oriented with head to the east and root to the west. The doorways themselves, which in the longhouses had the clan emblems mounted above them, constitute the crown and root chakras, while the five fires signify the other five main chakras of the spine. The tribal council fires of the five Iroquois nations, and where they were placed, thus represented the same chakras in terms of the Great Longhouse of the Iroquoian landscape, with the main Council fire of the Confederacy being the heart fire held by the Onondaga nation. (See figure 40, page 111; also note Plates 17 and 18, page 54.)

In the Iroquois landscape, the crown and root chakras are powerfully marked by Niagara Falls (root) and Mount Marcy (crown), the highest peak of the Adirondacks. The Seneca occupied the territory associated with the sacral chakra, and it is a matter of note that one of their main traditions concerns an island (Squaw Island) on Lake Canandaigua which is called the Birthplace of the Seneca Nation. This island, which was previously subject to rapid erosion (now halted), is unique in all the Finger Lakes. The other Doorkeepers, the Mohawks, had as their land the "head" of the landscape, their council fire signifying the brow chakra. They guarded the crown, the high peaks of the forested Adirondacks, as well as the Mohawk Valley. (The Adirondack region is now a beautiful and unique State Park encompassing one third of New York State.)

The territory inhabited by the Cayuga is associated with the solar plexus chakra of this Iroquoian landscape, while the countryside that was once the home of the Oneida relates to the throat chakra. To the Oneida belonged the sacred Oneida Stone, emblem of good speech (like *Petros*, "Stone," the Latin for Peter, the spokesman of Jesus' Apostles), now located at Utica. The ancient territory of the Onondaga, the Fire-

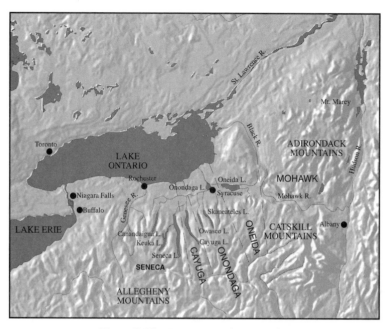

Figure 40. The "Iroquois" Landscape Temple.
From Mountain High Maps® Copyright © 1993 Digital Wisdom, Inc.
Used by permission.

keepers of the League, to whom was granted the privilege of keeping the League's Council fire, belongs to the heart chakra. This central fire was lit on a hill close to the Onondaga Lake, and represented the divine flame that shines in the heart of all creation. (See page 55, Plate 19.)

Linking the fires of the Five Nations was the "Ambassadors' Trail," the Iroquois highway, forming the axis of the landscape temple. This ancient trackway ran across the northern ends of the Finger Lakes, where the main tribal villages of the Seneca and Cayuga were located, and the southern end of Onondaga Lake, where the principal villages and fire hill of the Onondaga were situated. From the heart center of the Five Nations the highway extended to the Oneida's fire center just east of Oneida Lake, and then ran down the length of the Mohawk Valley, through the gateway of the Appalachians. A branch off this highway, instead of going down the Mohawk Valley, led up into the Adirondacks, up to what is now called Heart Lake (the geographical center of the

Adirondacks), close by Mount Marcy, the crown of the Iroquoian landscape temple.

SAN FRANCISCO BAY LANDSCAPE TEMPLE

One particular local landscape temple in North America which is working very creatively—not just for the United States of America but for the whole world—is that of the San Francisco Bay area. Not only do the Bay and its surrounding hills form a beautiful landscape, but the whole area is located on the great geological fault line, at the boundary of the Pacific and American tectonic plates, that runs the entire length of California's coastline. For some reason, such fault lines attract and energize people, while at the same time being potentially dangerous places in which to live. Unlike the landscape temple of the Iroquois nations, this one has not been consciously used and developed by people, but nevertheless its own inherent power and intelligence has influenced (and is still influencing) human activity sufficiently as to maintain and reveal the natural energy pattern in the large-scale human development of the area. (See figure 41.)

The Bay in fact lies between two fault lines, for the main fault line splits into two just south of the Bay, one line circumventing the Santa Cruz Mountains and San Francisco to the west, passing just offshore, and the other running alongside the Walpert Ridge and Berkeley Hills, which border the eastern side of the Bay. Further inland, the Diablo Range forms an eastern border to the area, the range culminating at its northern end with the solitary Mount Diablo. This mountain (1173 meters or 3849 feet high), standing out on its own in the landscape, is a major landmark for miles around and provides wonderful wide-ranging views from its summit.

To the west and across the Bay is Diablo's twin, the smaller but just as sacred Mount Tamalpais. In fact, both mountains were of special significance to the original native people of the area, who had a "volcanic story" concerning them and the making of the San Francisco Bay which is a key to understanding the landscape temple. The legend relates that Mount Tamalpais is the earthly form of a goddess whose brother, equated with the devil and Mount Diablo, once threw a rock at her in a rage. This great rock, however, fell short of the goddess and created the Bay. The rock (or a fragment of it) can still be seen, located between the two mountains just north of Berkeley. It is known as Indian Rock and is a place favored by many for watching the sun set across the Bay behind

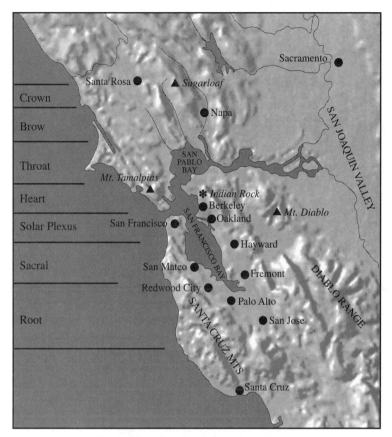

Figure 41. San Francisco Bay Landscape Temple.
From Mountain High Maps® Copyright © 1993 Digital Wisdom, Inc.
Used by permission.

Mount Tamalpais. (See Plate 20, page 56.)

This brief story, and the names of the two mountains, describe the significant polarity, left-right, of a landscape, with the heart stone between them. The gentle goddess, with whom Tamalpais is equated, is a traditional image of the right-hand side of compassion and mercy, while the Diablo or devil is a traditional image of the left-hand side of judgment and severity. The balance point between them indicates harmony—the heart point—and this center is located on the spine of the landscape.

Immediately to the east, running along the eastern side (*i.e.* the left side) of the landscape spine, are the Berkeley Hills and Walpert Ridge, while immediately to the west, lying along the western side (*i.e.* the right side) of the spine, is the Bay. The water and the hills make a good polarity with each other, their meeting point creating the balance or axis of the landscape temple. This polarity is further emphasized by the outlying regions: to the east, the Diablo Mountains, the San Joaquin Valley and the mountains of the Sierra Nevada; and to the west, the coastal region and the Pacific Ocean. The urban areas of Richmond, Berkeley, Oakland, Freemont, and San Jose lie along this spine, bordering the east bank of San Francisco Bay. Berkeley, with its university, is situated in the heart area of the landscape; the other towns are in the lower chakra areas, with San Jose in the root chakra.

These chakric areas are easier to identify to the west of the Bay, in the townscapes nestling between San Francisco Bay and the Santa Cruz coastline. For instance, situated in the sacral area, stretching from San Jose to San Francisco, is the world-famous Silicon Valley—an ideal location for such a creative industry. San Francisco, on the other hand, bathed in the energy of the landscape's solar plexus chakra, is, not surprisingly, famous for its wonderful restaurants as well as its dramatic locality. Not for nothing did the gold seekers rush here through the Golden Gate, for gold is emblematic of the sun as also of the ego— the ego which, in connection with the solar plexus, is equated with the lower self that is often (and naturally) desirous of fame and fortune.

The Ancient Egyptians equated the liver with the seat of the lower self in the human body, and the heart with the seat of the higher self. The two are, however, divided by a veil, or diaphragm, protecting the higher from the activity and possible misdemeanors of the lower. This veil is marvelously manifested in this landscape by the Golden Gate, the sea entrance from the Pacific into the Bay, which separates the city of San Francisco from the natural beauty of Tamalpais and its surroundings. (See Plate 21, page 56.)

Mount Tamalpais, focus of the right-hand aspect of the heart chakra on this western side of the landscape temple, is rightly protected as a State Park, as is its twin, Mount Diablo. Also maintained as a State Park is the small island in the Bay just to the west of Tamalpais, suitably called

Angel Island. Just south of Angel Island is the once notorious island of Alcatraz, but this lies in the "veil" of the landscape, not the heart.

Traveling further north we come to the throat area of the landscape, associated with the northern part of the Bay known as San Pablo Bay. At this point the Bay ends and the landscape transforms into hills and mountains with three main valleys cutting through them from the north, bringing three rivers southward to empty into the San Pablo Bay. Here begins the wine-making region, with its famous vineyards dotting the hillsides and valleys, and here commences the head of the San Francisco Bay landscape temple, with its brow and crown chakras. The brow area continues northward as far as the landscape's crown, marked by Sugarloaf Mountain, again protected as part of a beautiful State Park (Sugarloaf Ridge).

The mountains, of course, continue much further north, their peaks becoming higher and higher, and the vineyards of the lower southern slopes give way to majestic redwood forests. But it is in the vineyard area that the crown of this particular landscape temple lies, balancing, as its polarity, the city of San Jose at the southern end of San Francisco Bay.

A COUNTRY AS A
LANDSCAPE TEMPLE: ISRAEL

Israel, or Palestine, is a very powerful landscape temple, owing to its strongly contrasting polarities, and therefore a good example to give. The greater the polarities in any system the more difficult they are to balance, but the greater is the energy and creative potential. This huge energy potential explains why Israel has been so sought after, but also why historically it has been such a theater of turmoil in human affairs. Being so polarized itself, it tends to polarize people. As a land of great promise, it is worth striving for; but the blessings promised to the patriarch Abraham were entirely dependent on friendship between the various peoples who live in the land and adjoining it. Strife and friendship, or striving together in friendship, is the only way to achieve the blessings of the (or any) Promised Land! (See figure 42, page 116.)

As for the powerful polarities, first there is the major north-south polarity consisting of Mt. Hermon, the crown chakra, in the north, and the Dead Sea, containing the root chakra, in the south. Mount Hermon is so high that it is always capped with snow, providing the source of the River Jordan, the great river which flows southward all the way down the spine of the country, from the cold heights of the sacred mountain

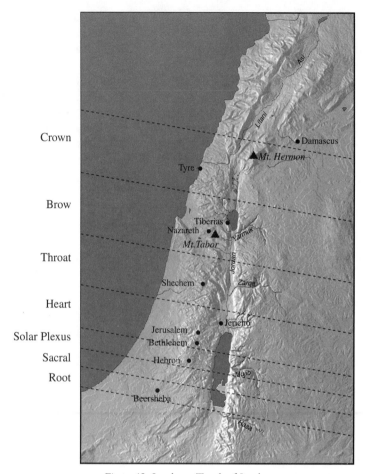

Figure 42. Landscape Temple of Israel.
From Mountain High Maps® Copyright © 1993 Digital Wisdom, Inc.
Used by permission.

to the hot depths of the Dead Sea. The Dead Sea lies so far below sea
level that it is exceptionally salty due to the evaporation of water in the
intense heat.

There is also a very strong east-west polarity. The spine of the landscape temple is double, with the Jordan in its river valley acting as one
pole, while the other consists of the range of hills stretched out parallel

to the river valley, along its west bank, on which the human settlements marking the chakras of the holy land are located. Thus the spine, itself, of the holy land contains the powerful polarities of a river valley and a ridge of hills, with a north-south orientation. In addition, the land to the west of the spine, toward the coast of the Mediterranean Sea, is relatively fertile, whereas the eastern side of the spine consists of arid desert. Bordering these, defining the east-west limits of the landscape temple, is the water of the Mediterranean Sea and the dry land of the Arabian Desert.

The chakras of the landscape temple are spread out from the root at the southern end of the Dead Sea and marked by Beer-Sheba ("The Seven Wells") at the edge of the spinal ridge of hills, defined by tradition as the southernmost limit of the holy land. The Dead Sea, originally and more correctly known as the Salt Sea, is an apt synonym for the divine Mother, Mary, whose name means "Salt Sea"—the "waters" of biblical tradition. The seven wells constitute another appropriate symbol of this material polarity to the lofty Mt. Hermon, representative of the divine Father—the "spirit" of biblical tradition.

Between Beer-Sheba and Hebron lies the sacral area. Hebron (meaning "The Friend") forms the solar plexus chakra, the principal seat of the lower ego and focus of personal power, where David first ruled as king over Judea, and which is today a major focus for the Palestinians.

At the heart lies Jerusalem ("The Great Peace"), the civil and religious center of the country, where the famous Temple of Solomon was built adjacent to King David's Palace, for the presence of God to dwell in. From this heart center both King David and King Solomon ruled, in turn, the whole of Israel. It is also where the great prophet-priest Melchizedek was king at the time of Abraham. With this great royal and religious center at their heart, the individual territories of the twelve tribes of Israel were disposed around the rest of the land, each tribe representing a sign or "creature" of the zodiac.

Just south of Jerusalem lies Bethlehem, traditionally the birthplace of the Messiah, later to be recognized (by his people) as rightful king in Jerusalem. Bethlehem ("House of Bread," or "House of Wisdom") occupies a position known in the Eastern chakra system as "the secret heart"; this is where the impulse of divine love is first born before it expands to fill the main heart chakra. This birth in the secret heart is enigmatically described as "the sound of one hand clapping."

The throat chakra, north of Jerusalem, is located at the ancient town of Shechem, which means "ridge." The settlement lies on a ridge between two mountains, Mt. Ebal in the north and Mt. Gerizim in the south, which are reminiscent of the two thyroid glands in the throat. According to Abraham's instructions, once a year the Israelites were to assemble at this place to promulgate the law, with six tribes gathered on Mt. Ebal and the other six on Mt. Gerizim. Between them, on the ridge, the Ark of the Covenant was placed. Those on the northern mountain were to chant the curses that would occur if the law was neglected, while those on the southern summit were to chant the praises that would accrue if the law was kept. In the time of Jesus, Shechem was the capital of Samaria; it is the only place where Jesus is recorded as saying that he was the Christ, when he spoke with the Samaritan woman at the well.

Further north, the brow chakra is marked by Mt. Tabor, whose impressive conical form is topped by an ancient citadel. Its shape reflects the pineal gland within the head, associated with the brow chakra. It used to be encircled by a group of small towns, one of which was Nazareth. Not far from there, as part of the River Jordan system, is the Sea of Galilee, also in the brow area.

Capernaum, on the north side of Galilee, and the adjacent Mount of the Beatitudes, is at the powerful "flash-point" (the center and source of the head halo) between the brow and crown chakras. Here Christ Jesus gave his main teachings, and it is still a place imbued with great light and spiritual energy. For the Jews, this area, and the area stretching northward, is the main center for the teaching of the Cabala.

At the crown chakra, the three snow-capped peaks of Mt. Hermon form a trinity. In Hebrew Cabala they represent the Ancient of Days, a synonym for the triple male aspect of God, the Holy Trinity. It was here that the Transfiguration of Jesus took place, and the vision of the three Masters (and much more) was experienced by the three senior disciples.

THE GRAIL KINGDOM TEMPLE

A landscape temple of great significance for the world covers the whole of Western Europe. It has a vital role to play in the world today as we enter the Aquarian Age and the beginnings of what will become a great Golden Age for humanity.

This important area of the world was once known as the Kingdom of Arthur, or the Grail Kingdom. The Arthurian legends are found throughout the Grail Kingdom, and are full of symbols relevant to the teachings of Zoence. The Round Table, with its twelve seats or places (and a mystical thirteenth in the center), represents a zodiac of time and space, as well as an ideal structure for human society and its evolutionary development. It also refers to the Wheel of Life and its spatial form, of which the zodiac forms a part. The Holy Grail—in Christian tradition the cup from which Christ drank at the Last Supper, although it also referred to his mother and to the land itself—was sought in quests by Arthur's knights. Finding the Grail and drinking from it is a symbol of illumination, and of the Golden Age to come.

The map (figure 43, page 120) indicates the pattern of the landscape temple. The spine runs approximately north-south down the center of Britain and France, with the head to the north and the root to the south. Each of the seven chakras can be visualized as a flower, a lotus, or rose of energy; they can also be perceived as the rungs of a ladder. They identify seven regions of France and Britain that are remarkably distinct from each other, almost like different countries, each manifesting the qualities and purpose of its particular chakra.

The landscape temple can be intuitively seen as a woman lying on her back with her head to the north, belonging to the earth while gazing up to heaven. She is the Queen, Guinevere ("the White Dragon," or "White Lady"), the Grail, itself, whom Arthur and his knights must love, protect, and serve, having first found and won her. Her love and knowledge is the wine that fills the Grail.

In the south the great mountain ranges of the Pyrenees and the Alps are like her pelvic bones. Between them lies the entrance to the womb, through the Golfe du Lion, the root chakra. Above this lies the Massif Central, with its volcanic *domes*, representing the sacral chakra and womb area.

Further north is found a totally different area of France, flat rather than mountainous, centered on Chartres. This represents the solar plexus chakra, whose energies influence northern France. Then comes the great divide, represented physically by the English Channel, which symbolizes the veil or diaphragm protecting the heart. The heart chakra, itself, is centered near London, at Kingston-upon-Thames with its landscape zodiac, but includes the whole London-River Thames landscape temple.

Further north in Yorkshire lies the throat area, with the alta major chakra in the borderlands of Northumberland—also with a vast

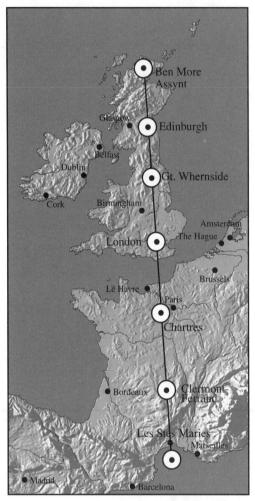

Figure 43. Grail Kingdom of Western Europe.
From Mountain High Maps® Copyright © 1993 Digital Wisdom, Inc.
Used by permission.

landscape zodiac and rich with Arthurian lore. The brow chakra, the
focus of vision and command, is centered on Edinburgh. (To those who
know both cities, the crisp, commanding character of Edinburgh is very
different from the more gentle quality that underlies London and its en-
virons.) In the very north of Scotland is the Assynt area, and in particu-

lar Ben More Assynt, which focuses and expresses the crown chakra energies.

A CONTINENT AS A
LANDSCAPE TEMPLE: EUROPE

The Grail Kingdom of Western Europe is part of a larger, continental landscape temple in which a myth is being acted out—a myth which gave the continent its name, and which exists to help explain the archetypal idea that is manifesting in the landscape. The continent is Europe, and the myth is the allegory of Europa and the Bull. The myth not only identifies the landscape temple, but also conveys deep knowledge concerning the role of Europe in the world, its evolutionary path, and eventual destiny, and how it affects the nations who inhabit her landscape. We can see this myth being acted out now with great intensity—politically, economically, and culturally.

There are several versions of this profound myth, handed down to us via the Greeks, but of a much older origin. The basic myth recounts how Zeus fell in love with Europa, the beautiful virgin daughter of Phoenix, the King of Phoenicia and Atlantis. But, in order to approach and woo Europa successfully, the great god had to take on the form of a bull and mingle with the herds of the Phoenix-King.

One day, when Europa was playing at the water's edge, gathering flowers with her companions, she saw the extremely handsome and shining snow-white bull. She was attracted by his gentle yet majestic beauty, and playfully approached the bull. She caressed the animal, wreathed flowers about its neck and horns, and gradually fell in love with the beautiful creature. The bull eventually knelt down and Europa climbed onto his mighty shoulders, whereupon the bull leapt into the air, spread its wings, and flew across the heavens.

Zeus, as the bull, carried Europa down to a secret place on Earth, and there they consummated their love. As a result Europa gave birth to Mercury, the golden child, and a golden age of wisdom, peace and prosperity ensued. (See Plate 22, page 57.)

An alternative version of the myth is usually told in the more popular books on mythology. In this version, Zeus lusts after the beautiful Europa rather than loving her. Europa is attracted to the bull and, once she has climbed onto its back, the bull swims across the universe to this Earth, carrying Europa off with him against her wishes. This time the bull has no wings and cannot fly, and the result of the affair is a rape rather than a love affair. No golden child or golden age ensues, only hurt and a barren land.

These two alternative versions of the myth—one a love affair and the other a rape—are important and were obviously composed deliberately by the creators of the myth. For instance, when the myth is seen as an allegory of human behavior under certain circumstances, the two versions show the two primary possibilities that might occur. Which will take place depends on us: the choice is ours.

A later and better-known Greek version of the myth attributes three children to Europa (Minos, Sarpedon, and Rhadamanthus) and attaches the myth to specific locations in the area of the Ægean, namely Crete, and to certain historical people and events. But the earlier pre-Greek version involves something archetypal which concerns the whole landscape of Europe.

Just as Zeus is represented by a bull, so the symbol of Europa is the dove, who is depicted in art as sitting on the shoulders of the bull. In the starry heavens, the Europa and Bull myth is portrayed by the constellation of Taurus, the Bull, on whose neck or shoulders sits the star cluster known as the Pleiades. In old star maps, as well as on coins and in pictures, sculptures, and pottery, the Pleiades are represented collectively by a dove that sits on the neck of the bull. The seven principal stars that compose the Pleiades star cluster are known as the Seven Sisters, or Doves, virgin daughters of Phoenix, King of Phoenicia, and his wife Pleione. Besides a single dove, these seven stars or "sisters" are also represented collectively in myth by a single star, reputedly the brightest and most beautiful in the heavens, called Maia, the Mother, from which is derived the name "Mary."

This story has its manifestation in the landscape of Europe. For instance, look perceptively at a map of Europe and you will see that the British Isles, together with Ireland, represent Europa, who is Maia—the name *Britanna* being a synonym for "Mary," and the islands being known in Catholic legend as "the Dowry of Mary"—while the rest of the European continent portrays the mighty Bull, head down and charging westward. (See figure 44.)

The head of the Bull is formed by Spain, while its powerful neck and shoulders are signified by France, on which sits Britain, the Dove. The horns of the Bull project as energies across the Atlantic from the crown of its lowered head. This crown chakra is marked by the famous

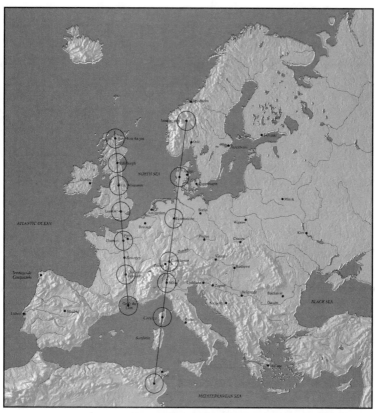

Figure 44. Landscape Temple of Europe.
Note the chakras of Europe, the Grail Kingdom axis, and the heart-line of
Europe. From Mountain High Maps® Copyright © 1993 Digital Wisdom, Inc.
Used by permission.

pilgrimage center, Santiago de Compostela, to which pilgrims have been journeying for centuries along the energy routes of Europe.

The brow chakra, represented by the eye of the Bull, is marked by Madrid, capital of Spain, while the throat chakra is centered on Bourges, the "heart" of France. Vienna acts as the main focus of the solar plexus chakra, and Belgrade the sacral. The root lies in the Black Sea, with the mountains of Rumania and Bulgaria, like the Alps and Pyrenees of the Grail Kingdom, acting like the pelvis of the Bull and guarding the gateway into the European landscape temple.

The Bull's great heart is located at Lake Constance, where the borders of Germany, Austria, and Switzerland meet, with the Swiss Alps on one side, and the Black Forest on the other. From the white peaks of the snow-clad Alps, the River Rhine has its beginnings, flowing first into Lake Constance and then traveling west and northward, mingling finally with the waters of the River Thames in the English Channel. The Rhine and Thames are like the bloodstreams from two hearts, the Bull of Zeus and the Dove of Europa, flowing together to become one.

Balancing the Rhine, the waters of the Danube rise from the subterranean depths of the Black Forest, flowing eastward through the lower body of the European Bull to its final outlet in the Black Sea. Furthermore, via an underground channel that emerges as the River Aach at Aach, at the western end of Lake Constance, the Danube is connected with the Rhine. White waters and black waters—these constitute two life streams passing through Europe from the great heart center of the Bull.

Fascinatingly, the diaphragm of the Bull is virtually located where the political and military division between Eastern and Western Europe used to be until 1990. The Bull's forelegs, described in legend as being "bent under," are defined by Italy and the islands of Corsica, Sardinia, and Sicily. Cicero referred to the Bull as being "on bended knee," and Manilius more accurately described this as the Bull "striving"—either in the sense of pulling the Plough (to which the Bull is said to be yoked), or in the sense of charging across the universe with Europa and sweeping away all injustice from the world.

The Bull's arched back is delineated by northern Germany and Poland; and its rump by the Eastern European countries of Rumania and Bulgaria. But, like the heavenly Taurus, the rear end of the European Bull is undefined. Star lore states that this is because the sign depicts the Bull emerging from the waves of the Great Sea, with Europa on his shoulders; thus his back legs are immersed in and hidden by the waves—in this instance, the waves of the Black Sea.

Echoing the constellation of Taurus in the heavens, the European Bull's head is lowered and his back is arched as he charges. This posture traditionally signifies the Bull sweeping away all injustice from the world; thus, in conjunction with Europa on his shoulders, he is "The Bringer of Illumination." The biblical description associated with Taurus is: "The Coming of the Lord in judgment to rule heaven and earth."

The whole astrological sign of Taurus and the Pleiades, wherein is found the cosmological story of Europa and the Bull, is associated with the establishment on Earth of a golden age of peace and illumination—a state of being which Europa's firstborn child, Mercury, personifies. This child is, in landscape terms, the Grail Kingdom of Western Europe.

Since Taurus rules the throat, the myth of Europa and the Bull identifies Europe's function in the world, as understood by the sages. Since the whole world is a Grail Kingdom on a larger scale, with its corresponding Grail King, then the planetary wound which Europe suffers is the one concerned with love. To heal this wound would be a great service for the world, and would begin the process of healing the planet and leading it toward a golden age.

THE EUROPEAN HEARTLINE

Within the landscape of the Bull of Europe there are many subsidiary landscape temples or chakra systems. One of them is especially significant, and may have something to do with enabling the Bull to fly.

In the good version of the myth the Bull has wings and flies; for Taurus, the Bull, is one of the winged Cherubs that guard the gates to Paradise. Wings are associated with the Holy Grail of knowledge and illumination, summarized by Shakespeare when he wrote that ignorance is the curse of God, knowledge the wing wherewith we fly to heaven (*2 Henry IV,* iv, 7). We only grow wings of light and fly with them when we have reached the state of joy or knowledge that is the result of love, understanding, and service. In landscape terms, the wings of the European Bull appear to be represented by Denmark, Sweden, and Norway.

Stretched out along the longitude 9°, from the western end of Lake Constance northward through Germany, Denmark, and the tip of Norway, and southward through Switzerland, northern Italy, Corsica, and Sardinia, is a great energy line which passes through some very significant sites. These sites form a chakric system on this energy line, with the heart chakra centered on the western part of Lake Constance, in the great heart of the Bull. For this reason the line is named the heartline of the Bull of Europe.

An actual island situated in the Untersee is the focus of this heart center of the heart-line—the famous island of Reichenau, home to three special churches that mark the heart, crown, and root of the island's landscape temple. Appropriately, the abbey church of St. Mary, in the heart of the island, houses a vial of the Sacred Blood of Jesus, and St.

George's Church at the crown of the island is home to the head of St. George. The church of St. Peter and St. Paul marks the root chakra.

The throat chakra of the Bull's heart-line is focused at the Externsteine, center of a 45-miles-in-diameter landscape zodiac and chakric system, and the place reputed to be the ancient focus of the Germanic folk soul. Further north, the line runs along the axis of the Jutland landscape temple, the powerful brow center of the Bull's heart-line, from where the Vikings took their worship of Thor and the Bull with them throughout Europe and even into America. Milan, in northern Italy, once known as the "New Athens" when it was the imperial headquarters of the Roman emperors, lies within the solar plexus chakra; while the sacral chakra is to be found focused in Sardinia. The crown of the line lies in the snow-covered mountains of Norway, and this is suitably polarized by the base of the line which is anchored in the desert mountains of Tunisia, homeland of ancient Carthage, the famous Phoenician trading center and a major gateway to the mysteries of Europe.

A CONTINENT AS A
LANDSCAPE TEMPLE: NORTH AMERICA

Strongly related to Europe as a landscape temple, through migration and the natural energy flow across the planet, is North America. Divided north-south into western and eastern halves by the great plains of the Missouri and Mississippi rivers, it stands as a magnificent example of a continental landscape temple. (See figure 45.)

The main feature of the western side of North America is the mighty range of the Rocky Mountains, stretching all the way from Alaska to New Mexico, and continuing further southward as the high Sierras of Mexico. Associated with the Rockies, in the United States, is the Sierra Nevada and Great Basin. Not only is this landscape higher than its eastern counterpart, but much of it is desert, baked by the fire of the sun.

Balancing this are the Appalachian Mountains of the eastern side of North America, topped in the north by the Great Lakes and, in the far north, by Hudson Bay. Unlike the desert or high mountain conditions of the western side, the Appalachians and eastern coast are heavily forested and filled with creeks, streams, rivers, and lakes. The polarity of this eastern part of North America with the western part is well illustrated by the contrast of the Great Lakes with the elevated Great Basin and Southern Rockies.

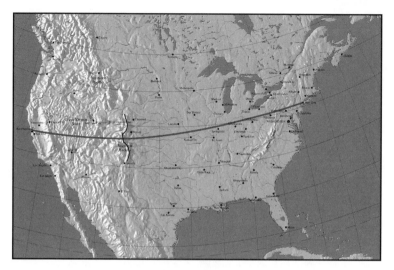

Figure 45. Landscape Temple of North America.
Showing the "horizon" energyline (the arrows) and the "bow" of the
Southern Rockies. From Mountain High Maps®
Copyright © 1993 Digital Wisdom, Inc. Used by permission.

Fire and water are natural polarities, as are high places and low places, mountains and lakes, sharp peaks and rounded peaks, desert and forest (or desert and garden, etc.). The west side of North America is clearly a "fire" side, and the east side is a "water" side. This is further emphasized by the culture that has arisen on each side of the continent. The east coast still retains its strong European connections, and expresses a marked emphasis on the marketing, organizing and administrative skills associated with the left side (or left hemisphere of the brain), as also with social convention. By contrast, the western side of America is linked far more to the pioneering spirit and is a cradle of creativity, imaginative ideas, passionate energy and liberality, all of which is related to the right side (or right hemisphere of the brain).

This polarity is well illustrated on the one hand by the outstanding examples of Los Angeles, home of the Hollywood film industry and Disneyland, and the San Francisco Bay area, home of Silicon Valley and the microchip. On the other hand there is Washington, DC, home of the government of the United States, and New York, city of bankers and

lawyers, and all kinds of commerce. These differences can be summarized in one great symbolic example, that of the United Nations, which
was created in San Francisco but is organized and run from New York.

Even civilization's unbalanced tendency for the "right" to be dominated, controlled, and possessed by the "left" is markedly shown in this
landscape, wherein so much of the land in the west of the United States
is owned or controlled by the Federal Government in the east, and
where the initial grid pattern land plots (associated with left-brain
thinking) and street layouts of cities in the west were laid down, irre-
spective of the contours and features of the landscape, by planners in the
east who never even visited the west.

The two sides or polarities need each other. They need their differences, as in all forms of life, but they also need to balance and harmonize
their differences. When working together in harmony, true prosperity is
created. The fundamental basis of this prosperity, in a material sense, can
be seen manifested in the vast and fertile land of America's central
plains, which has become the breadbasket not just of the United States
but also of many parts of the world that are in need. Symbolically, the
heart is represented in classical tradition by Demeter (Ceres) and her
daughter Persephone (Core), the great goddesses of Nature and growing
crops. This central area of North America manifests this spiritual archetype beautifully.

Just as the Mississippi and Missouri rivers mark the spine of the
North American landscape temple, a line stretched from San Francisco
to New York provides the "horizon," running through what would be
the central heart area in the vicinity of Mound City, between Omaha
and Kansas City, where it crosses the Missouri, and Hannibal on the
Mississippi, home town of Mark Twain. This energy line can also be dis-
covered to pass through the central and highest part of the Southern
Rockies, which form the shape of a bow in the landscape. The northern
part of this bow is even called the Medicine Bow Mountains! This bow
is stretched out from Santa Fe in New Mexico to Elk Mountain in
Wyoming. Its handle is represented by the highest peaks, such as Mt.
Massive, Mt. Elbert, and the other adjacent mountains stretching southward, which are all named after universities. The bow is an ancient symbol of the heart. The "horizon" energy line—the heart-line of North
America—is like its arrow. (See Plate 23, page 58.)

To the south of this horizon lie the lower landscape chakras—the
solar plexus, sacral, and root; while above it can be found the higher

chakras—the throat, brow, and crown. The latter two, forming the head of the continental landscape temple, would appear to lie in Canada, while the throat is situated in the northern part of the USA. The throat wound of the Grail King shows itself in the landscape (as it does so often throughout the world) in the border division between Canada and the United States.

For those who would like to analyze the continent further, the picture of three "pillars" can be superimposed on the North American landscape (*i.e.* left-hand, middle and right-hand pillars), as in Freemasonic and Cabalistic tradition, coupled with the further picture of the seven-runged ladder. The rungs of the ladder divide the landscape into chakric areas. The San Francisco/New York horizon, which would pass horizontally through the very middle of the ladder, can be taken as a guide to setting out the picture. With such a picture, a great deal more can be understood about the history and evolving culture of the North American people. Furthermore, its great emblem is the eagle, symbol of the brow chakra, for the continent forms the brow chakra of the planet.

Humanity and the Environment

Holy persons draw to themselves all that is earthly.
The Earth is at the same time mother.
She is the mother of all that is natural, mother of all
that is human.
She is the mother of all, for contained in her are the
seeds of all. —HILDEGARD VON BINGEN

LIVING IN HARMONY WITH OUR ENVIRONMENT

To live in harmony with ourselves and our environment involves much more than learning to live peaceably with each other without polluting the Earth that supports us, the water we drink, and the very air we breathe.

As we have seen, our environment ranges from our local landscape to that of our country, our continent, our planet, the solar system, the galaxy, and ultimately the universe. Each greater form includes the smaller forms within as part of its body. All these forms are exquisitely designed patterns of chakras and energy lines. None of this is haphazard, and these energy patterns within nature, together with their functions and influences, can be recognized as manifestations of universal law and order.

Since humanity is an integral part of this whole, the environment affects human consciousness, and our consciousness affects the environment. Wherever we are in these larger energy patterns of nature, we are fundamentally influenced by the energy of that part of the greater whole, and by the intelligent lines of flowing energy that connect each part in a web of life.

The influence of our environment is, by and large, subliminal. But even if we are not consciously aware of it, our subconscious is constantly affected by our surroundings, which can actually cause illness, depression, and disturbed behavior—or which can create and maintain good physical and emotional health, and creative behavior.

Thus, the siting of our village, town, or city can affect us for good or ill; so can the siting of our homes and work places. These days many of the detrimental factors prevalent in man-made environments are beginning to be recognized, but they are still too often ignored.

We do have some choices. For instance, our very position in a room has an effect on us. Many of us have preferred places where we like to sit, stand, or lie; if we enter a room and cannot occupy the place where we feel most comfortable, we can feel irritable and off-balance. Our position also affects our relationship with others in that room. Simply starting to be aware of your feelings under different circumstances, and doing something to make them feel better, will help you improve your relationships with your home, your family, friends, and your work environment. Moving to a more comfortable position (for you) in a room is usually such a simple affair. It is worth trying.

CREATING A TEMPLE IN YOUR OWN HOME

It is possible to discover a "temple" structure in your own home, by finding the chakras, and enhancing them so that your home becomes a healthy, inspiring, temple of life.

The kitchen is normally the sacral chakra, with the back entrance and any storerooms forming the root chakra. The dining area, whether separate to the kitchen or not, expresses the solar plexus chakra.

The main family room or living room is the heart of the house, sometimes also incorporating the throat area. The heart is the cosy area, where the family like to be and where they feel safe and intimate. Originally, this room would have the family fire burning on the family hearth—the heart, itself. In a large house, the throat chakra may be in an extra living room or music room leading from the main room. The throat areas are good for reading, studying, music, and discussions.

The brow area is also a good place for a study or an office, though in a small house the bedrooms will usually lie in the brow chakra, with the staircase possibly performing the function of the throat chakra. The crown area, if you are fortunate enough to have one, is a good place to have a small sanctuary or meditation room. This is also a good place to keep a light permanently burning; alternatively this can be kept in the heart chakra, in the main living room.

In a large house, you may find a complete chakra system on the ground floor, echoed by a second system on the floor above.

Whether your home is a house or an apartment, you will usually be able to find these areas; or you can create them, by being conscious of the chakras and their purpose. They do not have to follow a straight line; in fact they often don't, but it is vitally important that the chakras connect to each other in the right order, and that there is a flow of movement between them in the right order. The flow does not have to go directly from one room into the next; it can go via a hall or passageway. The important thing is that you don't have to pass through the living area when on the way from the kitchen to the dining room, or have to go through the kitchen to reach the bedrooms, etc. Much of this is common sense; what isn't realized is that there is a wisdom behind what works well, and it is important for our health and sanity, and for the health of the house, itself. (Houses, like all buildings and environments, build up their own atmosphere as well as character.) Disturbance and ill-health occur when there is a muddle, with a corresponding confusion of activities.

THE SANCTUARY

It is possible to set up a protected and harmonious space in a special room of your house (a crown chakra room is best), or indeed in any room, using a symbolic arrangement of the Wheel of Life. There are any variety of symbols that can be appropriately used; it is the thought behind them that is the vital factor, as everything is a manifestation of thought. There is plenty of scope for invention. Making a Wheel of Life, or Mandala, redistributes the energies in that room into the cosmic pattern of harmony and beauty. It can even affect the whole house and environment in a beneficial way.

The way to do this is to first establish the center or heart of the room. Mark it with something beautiful and meaningful—a flower, a candle, a beautiful stone, a crystal, are some things that work well. The perfect center will be composed of something that shows the male-female theme—a candle in a holder or floating in a bowl of water, for instance, or a vase of flowers. (In terms of flowers, the rose and lily are traditionally considered to be polarities, and yet both express the heart nature.)

Then work out which are the main directions, starting with the north, and decide which wall of the room represents north for you, and so on. Choose symbols for these directions based on the four main quarters of the Wheel of Life, which could be objects (*e.g.* a stone or bowl of seed for the north, a bowl of water for the east, flowers or incense for the south, fruit or a candle for the west); or colors (*e.g.* white for the north, blue for the east, yellow-gold or green for the south, rose pinks or red for the west) painted on mats, cushions, wall hangings, or symbolic paintings or ornaments. Place these symbols either on a central table or around the room, in such a way as to create a mandala of the Wheel of Life. You can go further and mark the quarter-directions as well, and the chakras of the room, but this simple arrangement of the center and four main directions is the basis, and it works.

Choosing and placing these symbols, when done with care, establishes the energy pattern of the Wheel of Life, which is a chakra or energy vortex. It creates a sacred space. Using the sacred space in a suitable and regular way then honors what it represents, and the "love-affair" begins, soul is created, harmony and beauty come into our life.

ORIENTATION

A factor that influences us subtly but powerfully is our orientation. We see what is in front of us: all our senses and awareness are geared in a forward direction. What is behind us affects our consciousness quite differently, as does whatever is to our left and right sides. When we speak to others, we usually face them in a particular way, squarely or at an angle, and are positioned at a certain distance from them. All of these factors can make a vital difference to our effect on one another, and whether or not we feel comfortable.

Business people are often aware of these factors: at board meetings and interviews the placing of the participants is usually carefully thought out. The organizers of functions also give a lot of thought to the seating at formal dinner parties or banquets. Otherwise, the question of orientation is rarely given any thought—yet it has a strong subliminal effect upon our psyches, and thus on our bodies.

If this surprises you, it is easy to become aware of it for yourself. Make a space in the room you are in, and assess how the walls are placed in relation to the north, south, east, and west. Lie on the floor, first with the head to the north. Then lie for a few minutes with your head in each of the other directions, and notice how you feel in each one. Most people easily sense the difference.

When you have tried them all, lie again for five minutes in the direction in which you feel most comfortable. Then, as a check, lie in the opposite direction and see how you feel. Then repeat the same exercise sitting or standing. You may find yourself changing the direction of your bed, desk, or other furniture as a result, to your benefit.

LIGHT CENTERS AND LEY-LINES

Many people today are becoming increasingly aware, in a new way, of what are called "light centers," places of natural and spiritual beauty which are centers of inspiration, healing, upliftment, and most of all love. They have a quality of peace and are imbued with spiritual power and energy.

These places are often served by groups or communities devoted to increasing the beauty and "light" of the center—usually through prayer, meditation, gardening, and community service—and to linking the center consciously with other light centers around the world.

Light centers form chakras in the landscape, either major or minor, which are connected by lines of communication constituting a network of energy. Each is a temple of light; when they are linked with each other around the planet they form a greater structure, a world temple of light.

The interconnecting lines between light centers are known as ley-lines. They are channels of energy and consciousness (the two are inseparable), some of which criss-cross the entire world's surface in geometric patterns, linking sites which have similar purposes. The more famous and beautiful are associated with recognized sacred sites, and are often marked by churches, temples, shrines, holy wells, and so on.

Sacred buildings, such as temples, churches, and cathedrals, always used to be sited at chakra points in a landscape. There was once a science concerning this known to the temple builders. The dedication usually reflected the function of the landscape chakra upon which the church was built, while the church in turn was designed to enhance the energies and purposes of the chakra and its surrounding landscape, to make it work better and more harmoniously, and become more alive. Churches sited on crown chakras were very often dedicated to St. Michael or St. Margaret, both of whom are "dragon-slayers." Heart chakra churches were nearly always dedicated to St. Mary, and occasion-ally to St. George. Churches dedicated to St. Peter, the "speaker" for the apostles, are usually found at the throat.

The ley-lines that linked these sites were apparent to many of our an-cestors. The straight Roman roads that still mark our countryside were built on ley-lines; many of them were previously marked and used by the Celts and earlier cultures. They not only provided direct routes be-tween centers of power, but because they were energy lines the troops who marched along them energized themselves as well as enhancing the ley-lines.

You do not have to become an architect or engineer to heal the en-ergy of the planet. Fortunately, a great deal of what is now negative and unhealthy can be transformed relatively easily into a positive life-giving influence. To move structures such as incorrectly positioned buildings, roads, and watercourses is not so easy, but there are ways of mitigating the problems until time allows for a proper change.

This can be achieved through a transformation of people's awareness and motivation, by encouraging all of us to recognize the energy pat-terns of the living Earth, by genuine care for the environment and by engaging in life-enhancing activities.

SEVEN

Serving the Planet—
Zoence in Action

~~~

The word is a living being, spirit, all verdant greening,
  all creativity.
This word manifests itself in every creature.
                              —HILDEGARD VON BINGEN

*When we consciously set about serving and healing the planet, we are si-
multaneously healing ourselves and our own lives. Zoence offers us practical ways of doing this. Zoence can be summed up as knowing the right
thing to do in the right place, at the right time, and with the right orientation. It is based on natural and ancient laws and principles which, when
successfully applied, bring balance, health, and happiness to both human
beings and nature.*

  *Zoence encourages us to be aware of our effects on the world about us,
and how our environment affects us. In order to become conscious media-
tors between heaven and earth we need to use all our efforts and awareness, and cultivate love in our lives and relationships. To turn a network of
energy into a network of light requires three things: love, intelligent understanding of the wisdom of that love, and loving activity. Zoence provides a
number of practical ways in which we can increase our ability to be loving,
sensitive, and aware in our everyday lives, in our relationships, homes, and
surroundings.*

FOLLOWING THE LIFE PROCESS

For healing both yourself and your environment, a good start is simply to become increasingly aware of yourself and your motivation, and the vital part you play within the cycles of space and time. In your daily actions, you can be aware of the cycle of desire-thought-action, and when you have a very strong desire to do something, immediately dedicate it to good.

You can also attune yourself to the great movements of time by acknowledging and celebrating the major festivals. You can do this alone, or in small groups at home, or with the larger community.

CELEBRATING FESTIVALS

In celebrations people come together in fellowship, sharing joy and laughter, and activities such as sport, games, drama, dancing, music, and feasting. Whether it is a family occasion, such as a birthday, or one of the major annual festivals, such as Christmas, a group celebration can produce good will and happiness, and everyone returns to daily life feeling more positive and even healthier. One of the best ways we could serve the planet would be to celebrate each of the principal festivals of the year. Reviving the ancient Solar Festivals could really bring the Earth to full life again.

In this, place is important. Festivals can, of course, be celebrated anywhere, but working in attunement with the major chakras of both time and space simultaneously (*i.e.* at the major chakras of the landscape, at the Solar Festivals), festivals could heal, revivify, and enlighten the whole planet in a powerful way. A science could be evolved concerning which places to use and when, in order to generate the most beneficial results.

The resultant release of the creative energies of joy, love, and light at the right times and places would have an immense influence upon the whole of the Earth's body and mind, and on all living beings—not least the people who gather to take part in these festivals. What benefits the Earth automatically benefits ourselves, spiritually, emotionally, mentally, and physically.

DANCE, MOVEMENT, SONG, AND CHANT

Sacred dance is akin to the creative movement of life, helping the consciousness of the dancer become one with Universal consciousness. Performed in the open air, it is also a means of energizing the land and working with nature.

Two examples of sacred dance that are used to good effect are the Circle Dance and Paneurhythmy. Circle dancing is a continuation of ancient traditions of community dancing, in which the participants became a moving wheel of joyful energy. The Universal Dances of Peace are developing this theme in a very special way.

Paneurhythmy was created by the Bulgarian Master Peter Deunov, in the mountains of Bulgaria earlier this century. Also performed in a circle or wheel, it is a way of moving in rhythm and harmony with nature, oneself, and others. It has been found to have profound beneficial effects upon physical health and the nervous system.

Creating sound is another enjoyable activity that can help to recreate, heal and transform the body. Sound is essentially the vibration of life energy as it moves through the cosmos. In its most perfect form it is known as the Word of God, the Word of Love, that creates all good things. Song and chant give form to the sound, enabling it to manifest and produce certain effects on both the mind and matter. They can directly affect the psyche of both human beings and nature, and can produce altered states of consciousness. Song is a direct way of opening the heart in love. Singing to nature is very healing and a loving thing to do, especially when we listen to nature singing back to us. Friendships are made this way.

MEDITATION, INVOCATION, AND PRAYER

Meditation is a level of love and focused consciousness which is totally at peace. The mind becomes still and able to reflect, see, and enjoy the pure light of truth. This enjoyment is a state of bliss.

Invocation is the act of calling on a higher force for assistance. When performed with love and trust, from a meditative state of consciousness, we can ask for the help of angels, which are aspects of divinity with special functions and powers.

Prayer is the natural culmination of meditation and invocation. It is a creative act of will, actively using the energies of love while in a meditative state of consciousness and working in cooperation with the great angels of love. Prayer should always be preceded by a period of careful preparation, followed by loving attunement and meditation. This process in fact forms a creative cycle of life, following the principles of Zoence. The key power points in making a good prayer are:

Dedication—to begin the attunement;

Visualization—to begin the meditation;

Invocation—to begin the prayer;
Thanksgiving—to end the prayer and complete the cycle.
The whole constitutes the science of prayer.

CENTERING AND PROTECTING YOURSELF

As you begin to develop the life process more consciously, you are likely
to become more sensitive, and it is useful to practice methods of center-
ing yourself, and protecting yourself against incompatible energies.

The Cosmic Cross

This can be done at any time, but it is helpful to do it each morning, before starting on the day's activities.

It is performed using a mantra, a visualization, and four deep breaths.
The words of the mantra, which are spoken silently, in your mind, are:

> **In the name of the Wisdom and the Love, the Justice and the infi-
> nite Mercy, of the one eternal Spirit. Amen.**

The accompanying breathing and visualization are shown in Table 3,
page 141.

Sealing the Chakras

To seal the chakras does not mean that you shut off the chakras completely, as they are constantly open and responsive to life energy, but this
technique protects you against disturbing vibrations or unwanted energies (for example, when traveling on crowded trains or in supermarkets).
It also strengthens the chakras, by reinforcing their natural energy pattern. It is useful to do at the end of a meditation, before returning to the
outer world, or before venturing out of your home and into a potentially disturbing or unusual atmosphere.

Visualize that you are drawing a cross of light within a circle of light
on each of your seven major chakras in turn, starting at the crown and
ending at the root chakra. Doing it this way, in this order, also helps to
ground you.

Quick Protection

Two instant forms of protection are to place your hands over the solar
plexus, as the monks used to do, and to protect the alta major chakra at
the back of the neck by turning up your collar or wearing a silk scarf.

Table 3. The Cosmic Cross

BREATH	WORDS	IMAGE
–	*In the Name*	Visualize the flame of light in your heart.
In	*of the Wisdom*	See the shaft of light going up from your heart through the crown chakra, high into the sky above.
Out	*and the Love,*	See a shaft of light going down from your heart deep down into the earth.
In	*the Justice*	Draw a line of light out to your left.
Out	*and the infinite Mercy,*	Draw a line of light out to your right.

You will now draw a circle round the cross you have created, starting from as far beneath your feet as you can visualize:

BREATH	WORDS	IMAGE
In	*of the one*	Draw the circle up your left side to the top of your head.
Out	*eternal Spirit*	Draw the circle down the right side back to your feet.
In	*Aaa—*	Concentrate the light of love in your heart.
Out	*-men!*	Fill the whole circle with light from your heart.

Sprinkling cold water over the back of your neck is also very cleansing after you have been in crowds or an unpleasant atmosphere.

PILGRIMAGE

Pilgrimage is an ancient art. Basically it is a search for truth, for self-knowledge, for enlightenment. It is also a way of caring for both the planet and society, by working with the energies of Earth and cosmos, in love.

The ancient centers of pilgrimage—places like Chartres, Canterbury, Rome, and Santiago de Compostela—are still powerful energy points. In the past they were constantly energized by the flow of pilgrims, as were the routes the pilgrims traveled. Whether consciously or not, the pilgrims of former times were benefiting both these routes and themselves. This is still true today when pilgrims and well-meaning tourists visit sacred sites, even if they are not fully aware of the ancient tradition which they are keeping alive.

Pilgrimage, particularly when undertaken with a sensitive awareness, some knowledge and a spiritual intention, works with the energy currents and chakras of the Earth in order to stimulate healing, transformation, and transmutation. It can be equated with acupressure on the energy meridians and acupuncture points, as well as with cleansing and re-invigorating the Earth's circulatory system. It is also a way of giving healing and revitalization through love and illumined consciousness to the chakras and nervous system of the planetary body.

Whether you visit a sacred site on your own or on an organized pilgrimage, you can use the experience to become conscious of the natural energies and chakras to be found in the landscape, and to discover ways of recognizing and working with them.

Sensing or seeing the patterns in the landscape, and comparing them to the energies of your own body and psyche, can help you realize the subtle and intimate relationships between yourself and nature. With this realization comes a growing perception and inner knowing of what sort of activity is appropriate in any place, in order to create and maintain a living harmony between humanity and nature.

Pilgrimage normally has a healing and transforming effect on those who take part. Some people can feel the actual flow of energy through the landscape chakras. This inevitably resonates with their own chakras, and many healings have taken place, both emotional and physical. People with problems relating to particular chakras have found such healings happening as they reach those chakra points in a landscape temple; but how one reaches those chakra points is important.

Love is an energy which moves other energies, and even matter, itself. A true pilgrim, working with love, moves the earth energy through the landscape from one chakra to another, helping to vivify the Earth and create patterns of light and fountains of energy that bring about the illumination of people and the planet. No one can take part in this without being personally affected; the pilgrim's own consciousness is raised, and he or she gains more understanding of life.

EIGHT

Joy

_Parabrahma (God) is everlasting, complete, without begin-
ning or end. It is one indivisible Being. In It is the origin
of all knowledge and love, the root of all power and joy._
—KAILYA DARSANAM

The basic philosophy of Zoence is simple: life—true life—is love, and is
meant for enjoyment. Polarity can be explained in two ways, as love and
the beloved, or as joy and the enjoyment of that joy. There is nothing
greater than, in love, to enjoy the presence and whole being of someone
else. That gives joy to the other person, who enjoys being enjoyed, and
that joy is returned, with interest, to the original person. As soon as you
give joy, you receive it; as soon as you receive joy, you give it. Joy simply
multiplies: it is infectious.

Similarly with nature: if we take time to enjoy nature, nature recipro-
cates by giving us back more joy; and the more we enjoy life, the more
conscious we become of its beauty and power. To live life well, with a
true consciousness of love, brings a deep realization which is joy. Joy illuminates; joy lights up both people and nature; joy _is_ light.

Joy, of course, has its polarity, sorrow, which must not be ignored. We
cannot experience joy without also experiencing the sorrow of the
world. It is right to grieve, for instance, at the cruelty that people inflict
on other human beings and on all the kingdoms of life, as well as the
imperfections of our own nature, thoughts, feelings, and actions. It is

important to allow ourselves to experience this sorrow and not to deny it. Without it there could be no true compassion, and compassion is an essential aspect of joy.

But compassion has the power to transform the situation. True compassion is love in action, with understanding—and this leads to joy.

An old adage says, love always wherever you are, whatever you do, and whoever you are with, and you will find joy. When we find our joy, we find our paradise. This is the purpose of life.

And then he saw that Brahman was joy;
And from joy all beings have come,
By joy they all live,
And unto joy they all return.
                          —Taittiriya Upanishad

Appendix
How Zoence Developed

Zoence is the culmination of many years of study, research, and practical experience by the philosopher-architect and mystic Peter Dawkins. Born in Edgbaston, Birmingham, in 1945, and gifted with an intuitive sensitivity and clairvoyance from a young age, during his childhood he developed a deep love and awareness of nature and the angelic world, and a growing sense of the energies inherent in the environment.

Educated at King Edward VI High School, Birmingham, in 1964 he went to St. Catherine's College, Cambridge, to study architecture. He graduated in 1967 with BA (Hons), followed by a further two years' post-graduate study for a Diploma in Architecture and MA.

Besides studying architecture and playing jazz, the environment and facilities of Cambridge enabled him to begin researching into other subjects which deeply interested him, such as comparative philosophy, religion, history, and sacred architecture, and especially the wisdom traditions, which have been a continuing study ever since. In 1969 he joined an architectural practice in Birmingham, qualified as an architect and became a member of the Royal Institute of British Architects.

In the summer of 1972 Peter joined an architectural practice in Edinburgh in order to be with his fiancée, Sarah Wendy, who was then a student at Edinburgh University. Their wedding took place at the end of March 1973. It was while living and working in Scotland, and practicing a spiritual discipline, that Peter experienced a series of visions of a revelatory nature, leading him directly to a specialized knowledge of landscape temples and their energies, and to the work he now does with people and the environment.

In the summer of 1973 his interests were expanded when he met Hope Brameld while on retreat at the White Eagle Lodge, renowned for its profound but gentle methods of spiritual healing and teaching, and of which Peter and Sarah were already members. Hope introduced Peter and Sarah to the work of the Francis Bacon Society, of which she was the Hon. Secretary. For Peter this was the start of many years of research into the work of Sir Francis Bacon and the Rosicrucians (Brethren of the Rose Cross), with whom Bacon was intimately associated. This in turn provided him with a major entrance into a much deeper level of the Western Wisdom Tradition, and a further path of initiation and training.

Another important influence entered his life when, in 1974, he met Sir George Trevelyan, founder of the Wrekin Trust educational charity, who was to become a good friend and mentor. He invited and encouraged Peter to give lectures, lead pilgrimages, and share his growing knowledge more publicly.

In 1976, Peter became a project architect to the Scottish Special Housing Association in Edinburgh and Glasgow, which culminated with his involvement in the early stages of the Glasgow Eastern Area Renewal and the Glasgow Inner City Redevelopment Project.

Following inner vision and guidance, in September 1978 Peter gave up his job as an architect in order to devote himself to the Baconian-Rosicrucian work and the Temple Science (later to be called Zoence), particularly with respect to researching and making known the truths about landscape temples and the planetary temple, and using this knowledge in a practical work of service that many people could participate in for the healing and enlightenment of the planet. He and his family moved to southern England to live for a time with the Seekers Trust, a community in Kent involved with spiritual healing and teaching, while the work was being prepared.

Later in 1978, a meeting with Stanley Messenger, who was researching certain aspects of Rudolf Steiner's anthroposophical work, was the signal to make the landscape temple knowledge more public and develop it as a work of service. Work with Stanley's group led to the formation of Gatekeeper Trust, which in 1983 became an educational charity dedicated to evolving a deeper understanding and care of humanity's natural environment and our relationship to it.

During these formative years, Peter also met several people (most notably the Marquis of Northampton) who, in 1980, were to help him found the Francis Bacon Research Trust, another educational charity, to research more deeply the wisdom as well as the philosophy and history of Bacon, Shakespeare, and the Rosicrucians, and to share the results publicly.

In the seventeen years between 1980 and 1997, helped by his wife Sarah, Peter has given over 600 seminars, lectures, workshops, and summer schools (ranging from two-week to weekend and one-day events) in the UK, Ireland, Germany, Denmark, Holland, Belgium, France, Switzerland, Spain, and the USA. He has led over fifty major expeditions and pilgrimages worldwide, including England, Scotland, Wales, Northern Ireland, the Republic of Ireland, France, Germany, Israel, Egypt, India, Brazil, and Peru. He has also written several books as well as writing for, and in some cases editing, a number of magazines and newsletters.

In 1988, Peter began to develop a training course for what he then called the Temple Science. His workshops in Germany, Britain, and other countries evolved into a specific course, while at the same time he continued to lecture and lead pilgrimages. In addition he began private consultancy work for personal and environmental healing— for individuals, communities, and businesses—including the design of new environments according to the principles of Zoence. In 1994 he gave the name Zoence to his teachings; it is a synthesis of all his studies, researches, discoveries, and experience over the years.

THE ZOENCE ACADEMY AND TRAINING COURSE

Peter Dawkins is co-Director of the Zoence Academy with his wife Sarah, and runs a Zoence Training Course in several countries. The Zoence Training Course is designed to help people develop their consciousness, sensitivity, and knowledge concerning themselves and their environment, leading to greater harmony and effectiveness in their lives, homes, and places of work. Peter also leads specially designed geomantic pilgrimages worldwide, and is available occasionally for private or business consultancy.

Tel : +44 1295-688185   *Fax:* +44 1295-680770
Email: secretary@zoence.com   *Internet:* www.zoence.com

GATEKEEPER TRUST

GT is a UK educational charity whose principal concern is with the art of pilgrimage and its potential for personal and planetary healing. GT develops this art through knowledge of landscape temples and earth energies. The Trust has its own membership and newsletter, publishes books and articles, and runs an annual program of sacred journeys, workshops, and other events.

Tel: +44 1295-688185
Email: secretary@gatekeeper.org.uk
Fax: +44 1295-680770
Internet: www.gatekeeper.org.uk

THE FRANCIS BACON RESEARCH TRUST

The FBRT is a UK educational charity established to research and make known the lives, philosophy, and wisdom teachings of Sir Francis Bacon, Shakespeare, the Rosicrucians, and others; and hence to discover a major gateway into the Western Wisdom Tradition. The Trust has its own membership and newsletter, publishes books and articles, and runs an annual program of seminars, pilgrimages, and other events.

Tel: +44 1295-688185
Email: secretary@fbrt.org.uk
Fax: +44 1295-680770
Internet: www.fbrt.org.uk

THE MERLYN TRUST

The Merlyn Trust, registered in Eire, is an educational charity established for the purpose of researching and increasing public understanding of mankind's harmonious coexistence with the environment and all living forms on Earth. The Trust undertakes and supports projects which enhance the quality of the environment. It supports and initiates research into folklore, mythology, history, earth energies, and the Wisdom traditions, and pilgrimage both in Ireland and other parts of the world.

The Merlyn Trust, 7 Mount Eagle Grove, Foxrock
Dublin 18, Ireland.
Tel & Fax: +353 1-2957-351
Email: emerald@iol.ie

Index